VOGUE
CLASSIC
KNITS

Christina Probert

ANGELL EDITIONS

Newton Abbot, Devon

Acknowledgements

Colour photographs by Mario Testino 21, 49, 51, 62; Anthony Crickmay 4, 6, 9, 12, 15, 16, 19, 35, 40/1, 45, 47, 56, 58; Perry Ogden 11, 23, 26, 29, 31, 32, 37, 43, 53, 61.
Black and white photographs: Scavullo 5; Himmel 13; Ogden 24, 50; Silverstein 33; Donovan 55; Zatecky 63. Colour details: Dudley Montney 8, 17; Steve Kibble 10. Charts by Andy Ingham. Drawings by Barbara Frith and Marion Appleton.

Hair and make-up by Pat Lewis for Vidal Sassoon and Teresa Fairminer on pages 4, 9, 12, 16, 19, 40/1, 47, 53, 58; by Trevor at Colombe and Arianne 6, 15, 45; by Nicky Clarke and Ashley Russell, both of John Frieda, and Mark Hayes 11; by Mitch Barry and Leslie Chilkes 21; by Kerry Warn and Fran Cooper both of New York 23, 26, 29, 31, 32, 37, 43, 61; by Pascal 35, 56; by Orbie and Kevin 49, 62; by Mitch Barry and Mark Borthwick 51.

Clothes and accessories by Armani, Laura Ashley, Sheridan Barnett, Basile, Benetton, British Shoe Corporation, Brooks Brothers, Browns, Butler & Wilson, Comme des Garcons, Lawrence Corner, Paul Costello, Courtney, Crolla, Dickens & Jones, Perry Ellis, Fenn Wright & Manson, Fenwicks, Flip, Margaret Howell, Herbert Johnson, Katharine Hamnett, Harrods, Hennes, Herbert Johnson, Hobbs, Joseph, Kenzo, Kir, Calvin Klein, Lana Lino, Liberty, New & Lingwood, Mary Quant, John Marks, Maxmara, Mulberry, Options at Austin Reed, Benny Ong, Maxfield Parish, N. Peal, Andre Peters, Pollen, Marco Polo, Ralph Lauren, Russell & Bromley, The Scotch House, Sacha, Sunarma, Paul Smith, Tessiers, Tatters, Charles de Temple, Patricia Underwood, Whistles, The White House, Walkers, Zoran. International Textile Care Labelling Code courtesy of the Home Laundering Consultative Council.

British Library Cataloguing in Publication Data

Probert, Christina
  Vogue classic knits. – (Vogue knitting; 1)
  1. Knitting – Patterns
  I. Title   II. Series
  646.4'304   TT820

ISBN 0-948432-15-2

Printed in the Netherlands by Royal Smeets Offset, Weert for Angell Editions Limited Newton Abbot, Devon

Contents

PATTERNS

V-neck, Tri-colour Striped Cardigan 1959

Striped V-neck cardigan with three-quarter length sleeves, hemmed cuffs and lower edge, and doubled, separate front bands

★ Suitable for beginners

MATERIALS

Yarn
Wendy DK
3 × 50g. balls Col. A (Blue)
4(5:5:5) × 50g. balls Col. B (White)
4(4:5:5) × 50g. balls Col. C (Red)

Needles
1 pair 3¼mm.
1 pair 4mm.

Buttons
5

MEASUREMENTS

Bust
82(87:92:97) cm.
32(34:36:38) in.

Length
57(58:60:61) cm.
22¼(22¾:23½:24) in.

Sleeve Seam
36 cm.
14 in.

TENSION

24 sts. and 32 rows = 10 cm. (4 in.) square over stocking stitch on 4mm. needles. If your tension square does not correspond to these measurements, adjust the needle size used.

ABBREVIATIONS

k.=knit; p.=purl; st(s).=stitch(es); inc.= increase; dec.=decrease; beg.=begin(ning); rem. = remain(ing); rep. = repeat; alt. = alternate; tog. = together; sl. = slip stitch (transfer one stitch from left needle, knit-wise unless otherwise stated, to right hand needle.); cont. = continue; patt. = pattern; foll. = following; folls. = follows; mm. = millimetres; cm. = centimetres; in. = inch(es); st.st. = stocking stitch; A = colour A; B = colour B; C = colour C.

BACK

Cast on 102(108:114:120) sts. with 3¼mm. needles using A and work in st.st. stripes throughout, working 9 rows for this stripe, ending with a k. row.
Next row: k. to mark hemline.
Change to 4mm. needles and work as folls.:
*10 rows A, 10 rows B, 10 rows C, 10 rows B.
Rep. from * throughout. At the same time, inc. 1 st. at each end of 32nd row from beg. and foll. 12th rows until there are

108(114:120:126) sts.
Work to the end of 12th stripe when work should measure 41 cm. (16 in.).

Shape Armholes
Cast off 3 sts. at beg. of next 2 rows and dec. 1 st. at each end of foll. 3 alt. rows.
Cont. to keep stripe sequence correct and when back measures 57(58:60:61) cm. (22¼(22¾:22½:24) in.), cont. as folls.:

Shape shoulders
Cast off 10 sts. at beg. of next 6 rows and 2(4:6:8) sts. at beg. of foll. 2 rows.**
Work neckband on rem. sts. in A.
Work 10 rows, ending with a p. row.
Change to 3¼mm. needles, p. into back of each st. on next row to mark hemline.
Work 9 rows. Cast off.

LEFT FRONT

Cast on 49(52:55:58) sts. with 3¼mm. needles using A and work as for back, changing to 4mm. needles after hem, as for back.
Inc. 1 st. at beg. of 32nd row from beg. and every foll. 12th row until there are 52(55:58:61) sts.
Cont. to last row of 11th stripe.

Shape Neck and Armhole
k. to last 2 sts., k.2 tog. Work 3 rows in st.st.
Cont. to shape at front edge on every 4th row until there are 32(34:36:38) sts.
At same time, when front measures same as back to armholes, ending at side edge, shape armhole as for back.
After shaping, cont. to keep armhole edge straight.
When front measures same as back to shoulder, end at side edge.

Shape Shoulder
Work as for back to**.

RIGHT FRONT

Work as for left front, reversing shapings.

SLEEVES

Cast on 54(56:58:60) sts. with 3¼mm. needles using C and work in stripes as for back, changing to 4mm. needles after hemline.
Inc. 1 st. at each end of 8th row after cuff is worked (same as back hem) and at each end of foll. 8th rows until there are 76(78:80:82) sts.
Work straight until sleeve measures 36 cm. (14 in.).

Shape top
Cast off 3 sts. at beg. of next 2 rows and

dec. 1 st. at each end of foll. 3 rows.
Then dec. 1 st. at each end of every alt. row until there are 36 sts.
Now dec. 1 st. at each end of foll. rows until there are 24 sts. Cast off.

FRONT BANDS

With right side facing, beg. at top of left front and with 3¼mm. needles using A, pick up and k. 56(58:60:62) sts. down to front shaping and 90 sts. down to hemline.
Work in st.st. for 10 rows, work hemline as before and work a further 10 rows. Cast off.
Work right band to match starting to pick up and k. sts. from hemline, and working double buttonholes as positions are reached on right front as folls.:
4th row: k.5, cast off 3 sts., *k.18, including st. already on needle, cast off 3 sts., rep. from * 3 times more.
Next row: cast on 3 sts. over those cast off in previous row. Work 5 rows, then hemline row and a further 5 rows.
Now work a 2nd buttonhole row and foll. row similarly. Complete band.

MAKING UP

Press pieces. Sew up shoulder and neckband seams. Fold band to wrong side and catch down neatly using slipstitch.
Set in sleeves and sew up side and sleeve seams.
Neaten buttonholes. Sew on buttons and press seams.

Fluffy, Dolman-sleeved Sweater

Waist-length, stocking stitch, dolman sweater worked in two pieces, with elbow-length sleeves, ribbed welts and bands, and round neck

MATERIALS

Yarn
Pingouin Oued
4(4:5:5) × 50g. balls

Needles
1 pair 3mm.
1 pair 3¾mm.

MEASUREMENTS

Bust
82(87:92:97) cm.
32(34:36:38) in.

Length (to top of shoulder)
52(53:53:54) cm.
20½(20¾:20¾:21¼) in.

TENSION
24 sts. and 32 rows = 10 cm. (4 in.) square over stocking stitch on 3¾mm. needles. If your tension square does not correspond to these measurements, adjust the needle size used.

ABBREVIATIONS
k.=knit; p.=purl; st(s).=stitch(es); inc.= increase; dec.=decrease; beg.=begin(ning); rem. = remain(ing); rep. = repeat; alt. = alternate; tog. = together; sl. = slip stitch (transfer one stitch from left needle, knit-wise unless otherwise stated, to right hand needle.); cont. = continue; patt. = pattern; foll. = following; folls. = follows; mm. = millimetres; cm. = centimetre(s); in. = inch(es); st.st. = stocking stitch.

BACK
Cast on 80(86:92:98) sts. with 3mm. needles and work 9 cm. (3½ in.) in k.1, p.1 rib.
Change to 3¾mm. needles and st.st. Work 4 rows.

Inc. 1 st. at each end of next and every foll. 4th row until there are 104(110:116:122) sts.
Now inc. 1 st. at each end of alt. rows 4 times, then cast on 2 sts. at beg. of next 6 rows, 12 sts. at beg. of next 2 rows, and 14 sts. at beg. of next 8 rows. [260(266: 272:278) sts.]
Now cont. without shaping until sleeve edges, after the last casting on, measure 14(15:15:16) cm. (5½(5¾:5¾:6¼) in.) ending with a purl row. **

Shape Shoulder
Cast off 10 sts. at beg. of next 16 rows, 11(12:12:13) sts. at beg. of next 4 rows, and then 11(12:14:15) sts. at beg. of next 2 rows.
Cut yarn and place rem. 34(34:36:36) sts. on a holder.

FRONT
Work as for back to **.

Shape Shoulder and Neck
Cast off 10 sts. at beg. of next 6 rows.
Next row: cast off 10 sts., k. until there are 83(86:88:91) sts. on right needle. Turn, and complete this side first.
*** *1st row:* cast off 3 sts., p. to end.
2nd row: cast off 10 sts., k. to end.
3rd row: cast off 2 sts., p. to end.
4th row, 6th row and *8th row:* as 2nd row.
5th row: as 3rd row.
7th row: cast off 1 st., p. to end.
9th row: and 11th row: as 7th row.
10th row: cast off 11(12:12:13) sts., k. to end.
12th row: as 10th row.
13th row: p.
Cast off rem. 11(12:14:15) sts. ***
Now return to sts. left unworked.
Slip next 14(14:16:16) sts. onto holder.
Rejoin yarn to sts. of right front and knit to end.
Cast off 10 sts. at beg. of next row, p. to end.
Complete as for left front from *** to ***

reversing shapings by reading p. for k., and k. for p.

NECKBAND
Sew up right shoulder and upper sleeve seam.
With right side of work facing, using 3mm. needles, pick up and k. 23 sts. down left front neck edge.
Now, working sts. from front holder, k.1(1:2:2), [inc. 1 st. in next st., k.1] 6 times, k.1 (1:2:2), then pick up and knit 23 sts. up right front neck edge, then work-ing back neck sts., k.3 (3:4:4), [inc. 1 st. in next st., k.2] 10 times, k.1 (1:2:2). [110(110:114:114) sts.]
Work in k.1, p.1 rib for 3 cm. (1¼ in.). Cast off loosely ribwise. (see page 169.) Sew up shoulder and upper sleeve seam.

CUFFS
With right side of work facing, with 3mm. needles, pick up and k. 80(86:86:92) sts. along one sleeve edge.
Work in k.1, p.1 rib for 5 cm. (2 in.). Cast off loosely ribwise.
Work other cuff similarly.

MAKING UP
Sew up side and underarm seams. Press seams lightly on wrong side with warm iron and damp cloth.

Scarf-neck Fine Lace Blouse

Just below waist-length fine wool lacy blouse with ribbed welts, scarf neck in garter stitch, and set-in sleeves

MATERIALS

Yarn
Rowan Botany 3 ply
11(11) × 25g. balls.

Needles
1 pair 2¼mm.
1 pair 3mm.

MEASUREMENTS

Bust
84(89) cm.
33(35) in.

Length
53 cm. (20¾ in.)

Sleeve Seam
46 cm. (18 in.)

TENSION
32 sts. and 40 rows = 10 cm. (4 in.) square over stocking stitch on 3mm. needles. If

your tension square does not correspond to these measurements, adjust the needle size used.

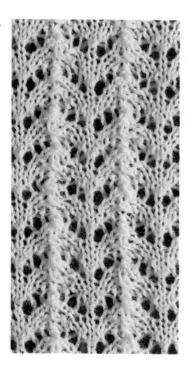

BACK

** Cast on 134(138) sts. with 2¼mm. needles, and work in rib as folls.:
1st row: (right side): k.2, * p.2, k.2, rep. from * to end.
2nd row: p.2, * k.2, p.2, rep. from * to end.
Rep. these 2 rows until back measures 8 cm. (3¼ in.), ending with a 2nd row.
Now work in k.1, p.1 rib until back measures 13 cm. (5 in.), ending with *wrong* side facing for next row.
Next row: rib 15(9), m.1, (rib 26(15), m.1) 4(8) times, rib to end. [139(147) sts.]
Change to 3mm. needles and work in patt. as folls.:
1st row (right side): sl. 1k., k.1, * y.fwd., k.2, sl. 1k., k.2 tog., p.s.s.o., k.2, y.fwd., k.1, rep. from * to last st., k.1.
2nd row: sl. 1p., p. to end.
3rd row: sl. 1k., k.2, * y.fwd., k.1, sl. 1k., k.2 tog., p.s.s.o., k.1, y.fwd., k.3, rep. from * to end.
4th row: as 2nd.
5th row: sl. 1k., k.3, * y.fwd., sl. 1k., k.2 tog., p.s.s.o., y.fwd., k.5, rep. from * to last 7 sts., y.fwd., sl. 1k., k.2 tog., p.s.s.o., y.fwd., k.4.
6th row: as 2nd.
These 6 rows form patt.
Cont. in patt. until back measures 33(34) cm. (13(13¼) in.), ending with right side facing for next row.

Shape Armholes

Cast off 8 sts. at beg. of next 2 rows, keep-ing continuity of patt.**
Dec. 1 st. at each end of next and every foll. alt. row until 109(119) sts. rem.
Work straight until back measures 53 cm. (20¾ in.), ending with right side facing for next row.

Shape Shoulders

Cast off 7(8) sts. at beg. of next 6 rows, then 8 sts. at beg. of next 2 rows.
Cast off rem. 51(55) sts.

FRONT

Work as for back from ** to **.

Divide for Neck

Next row: k.2 tog., patt. 57(61), k.2 tog., turn and leave rem. sts. on a spare needle.
Work 1 row.
Dec. 1 st. at each end of next and every foll. alt. row until 47(53) sts. rem.

Dec. 1 st. at neck edge *only* on every foll. alt. row from previous dec. until 39(44) sts. rem. Work 2 rows.
Dec. 1 st. at neck edge on next and every foll. 3rd row until 29(32) sts. rem.
Work straight until front matches back to start of shoulder shaping, ending with right side facing for next row.

Shape Shoulder

Cast off 7(8) sts. at beg. of next and foll. 2 alt. rows, keeping continuity of patt. Work 1 row, cast off rem. 8 sts.
With right side facing, rejoin yarn to rem. sts., cast off 1 st., patt. to end.
Work to match front side, reversing shap-ings.

SLEEVES

Cast on 54(58) sts. with 2¼mm. needles, and work in k.2, p.2 rib as on back for 6 cm. (2¼ in.), ending with a 1st row.
Next row: rib 3(5), m.1, (rib 4(3), m.1) 12(16) times, rib to end. [67(75) sts.]
Change to 3mm. needles and work in patt. as for back, shaping sides by inc. 1 st. at each end of 7th and every foll. 8th row until there are 103(109) sts., taking inc. sts. into patt.
Work straight until sleeve seam measures 46 cm. (18 in.), ending with right side facing for next row.

Shape Top

Cast off 6 sts. at beg. of next 2 rows, keep-ing continuity of patt.
Dec. 1 st. at each end of next and every foll. 4th row until 85(93) sts. rem. Work 1 row.
Dec. 1 st. at each end of next and every foll. alt. row until 57 sts. rem.
Work 1 row. Cast off.

MAKING UP

Omitting ribbing, press work lightly on wrong side following instructions on the ball band. Sew up shoulder, side and sleeve seams. Insert sleeves.

TIE

Cast on 3 sts. with 3mm. needles and work as folls.:
1st row (wrong side): k.1, m.1, k. to end.
2nd row: sl. 1k., k. to end.
Rep. these 2 rows until there are 25 sts.
Work straight until tie measures 100 cm. (39 in.), ending with *wrong* side facing for next row.
Next row: k.1, k.2 tog., k. to end.
Next row: sl. 1k, k. to end.
Rep. last 2 rows until 3 sts. rem. Cast off.
With right side facing and leaving 25 cm. (9¾ in.) free at each end of tie, join right side edge neatly up right side of neck, across back and down left side of neck.
Press seams.

Harlequin Sweater

Long, diamond-patterned, circular-knitted, V-neck sweater with sleeves worked downwards from picked-up armhole stitches

★★★ Suitable for experienced knitters

MATERIALS

Yarn
Templeton's H & O Shetland Fleece
7(7:8:8) × 25g. balls (Main Col. A)
7(7:8:8) × 25g. balls (Contrast Col. B)

Needles
1 set of 4 double-pointed 3mm. (ribbing)
1 circular 3mm. (ribbing)
1 set of 4 double-pointed 3¼(3¾:3¼:3¾)mm. (sleeves)
1 circular 3¼(3¾:3¼:3¾)mm. (body)
1 pair 3¼(3¾:3¼:3¾)mm. (upper body)

MEASUREMENTS

Bust
87(92:97:102) cm.
34(36:38:40) in.

Length
61(61:65:65) cm.
24(24:25½:25½) in.

Sleeve Length
45(45:47:47) cm.
17¾(17¾:18½:18½) in.

TENSION
Approx. 27 sts. = 10 cm. (4 in.) over patt. on 3¾mm. needles. Approx. 28 sts. = 10 cm. (4 in.) over patt. on 3¼mm. needles. If your tension does not correspond to these measurements, adjust the needle size used.

ABBREVIATIONS
k.=knit; p.=purl; st(s).=stitch(es); inc.= increase; dec.=decrease; beg.=begin(ning); rem. = remain(ing); rep. = repeat; alt. = alternate; tog. = together; sl. = slip stitch (transfer one stitch from left needle, knit-wise unless otherwise stated, to right hand needle.); cont. = continue; patt. = pattern; foll. = following; folls. = follows; mm. = millimetres; cm. = centimetres; in. = inch(es); st.st. = stocking stitch; t.b.l. = through back of loop.

FRONT AND BACK (worked together)
Cast on 252(258:282:288) sts. with 3mm. circular needle and B.
Join into a circle, placing a contrast yarn marker at join, and work in rounds to arm-holes as folls.:

1st round: with B, * k.4, p.2, rep. from * to end.
2nd round: with A, * k.4, p.2, rep. from * to end.
Rep. these 2 rounds until rib measures 5 cm. (2 in.), ending with a 1st round.
Change to 3¼(3¾:3¼:3¾)mm. circular needle and cont. in st.st.
N.B.: *All* st.sts. and patt. sts. are k. sts. when worked in the round.
1st round: with A, k.
2nd round: with B, k., inc. 14(8:12:6) sts.

evenly on round. [266(266:294:294) sts.]
Cont. in 2 col. patt.
1st round: * 1A, 1B, rep. from * to end.
2nd round: * 1B, 1A, rep. from * to end.
3rd round: * 1A, 1B, 3A (1B, 1A) twice, 3B, 1A, 1B, rep. from * to end.
4th round: * 1B, 5A, 1B, 1A, 5B, 1A, rep. from * to end.
5th round: * 7A, 7B, rep. from * to end.
6th round: as 4th round.
7th round: as 3rd round.
8th round: as 2nd round.
These 8 rounds form the patt. and are repeated throughout.
Cont. in patt. until work measures 41(42:43:44) cm. (16(16½:16¾:17¼) in.) or required length to armhole.
Slip next 10(10:8:8) sts. to right needle tip, rejoin yarn to next st. and cast off 8(8:12:12) sts. for left armhole, patt. a further 131(131:141:141) sts. for front, cast off next 8(8:12:12) sts. for right armhole and patt. a further 117(117:127:127) sts. for back. [132(132:142:142) sts. in front; 118(118:128:128) sts. in back].

Work Back
With 3¼(3¾:3¼:3¾)mm. needles, cont. on back sts., working in rows.
N.B.: When working on 2 needles, all wrong side patt. rows are p., all right side patt. rows are k.
Keeping patt. correct, work 56(56:64:64) rows.
Cast off.

Work Front
With wrong side of rem. sts. facing, rejoin yarn and cont. in patt.
Work 1 row.
Keeping patt. correct, dec. 1 st. at each end of next and every alt. row until there are 118(118:128:128) sts.
Work 1(1:5:5) rows more.

Divide for Neck
1st row: patt. 59(59:64:64), turn and complete left side of neck, leaving rem. sts. on holder.
Keeping patt. correct, dec. 1 st. at centre front edge on next 8 rows, then on every right side row until there are 39(39:42:42) sts.
Work 9 rows.
Cast off.
With right side facing rejoin yarn to rem. sts. for right side of neck and work to correspond with left side, reversing shapings.
Sew up shoulder seams.

SLEEVES

With right side of armhole facing and set of 3¾(3¾:3¼:3¾)mm. needles, beg. at underarm and using A and B alternately, k. up 112(112:126:126) sts. evenly round armhole and arrange on 3 needles, marking end of round as for body. Work in rounds of two col. patt. as for body, beg. with a 2nd row.
Work 1 complete patt.
Cont. keeping patt. correct, dec. 1 st. at each end of next and every 8th round until 102(102:116:116) sts. rem., then dec. 1 st. at each end of every 4th round until there are 70(70:84:84) sts.
Cont. until sleeve measures 40(40:42:42) cm. (15¾(15¾:16½:16½) in.) or 5 cm. (2 in.) less than required finished sleeve length.
Next round: with B, k.
Next round: with A, k., dec. 22(16:24:24) sts. evenly. [48(54:60:60) sts.]
Change to set of 3mm. needles.
Now work 5 cm. (2 in.) cuff in rib patt. as given at start of body. Cast off loosely.

NECKBAND

With set of 3mm. needles and B, and with right side of neck facing, k. up 50(50:54: 54) sts. down left side of neck, with 2nd needle k. up 50(50:54:54) sts. up right side of neck, and with 3rd needle k. up 42(42:46:46) sts. from back. [142(142:154:154) sts.]
1st round: 1st needle – * k.2, p.2, rep. from * to last 2 sts., k.2 tog., 2nd needle – k.2 tog. t.b.l., * p.2, k.2, rep. from * to end, 3rd needle – p.2, * k.2, p.2, rep. from * to end. Keeping rib as set, work 3 more rows, dec. at end of 1st needle and beg. of 2nd needle on each round as for 1st round.
Cast off loosely in rib, working centre front dec. on this row also.

MAKING UP

Roll finished work in damp towel and leave for 1 hour. Pin out to size. Leave until dry before unpinning.

Boat-neck Dolman Sweater

Two-tone simple dolman sweater with hem, neck facing and three-quarter length sleeves worked all-in-one with body, in stocking stitch

★ Suitable for beginners

MATERIALS

Yarn
Sirdar Country Style 4 ply
7(7:7:7:8) × 50g. balls (Main Colour)
2(2:2:2:3) × 50g. balls (Contrast Colour)

Needles
1 pair 2¾mm.
1 pair 3¼mm.

MEASUREMENTS

Bust
82(87:92:97:102) cm.
32(34:36:38:40) in.

Length
60(61:62:63:64) cm.
23½(24:24¼:24¾:25) in.

TENSION

14 stitches and 18 rows = 5 cm. (2 in.) square over stocking stitch on 3¼mm. needles. If your tension square does not correspond to these measurements, adjust the needle size used.

ABBREVIATIONS

k.=knit; p.=purl; st(s).=stitch(es); inc.= increase; dec.=decrease; beg.=begin(ning); rem. = remain(ing); rep. = repeat; alt. = alternate; tog. = together; sl. = slip stitch (transfer one stitch from left needle, knitwise unless otherwise stated, to right hand needle.); cont. = continue; patt. = pattern; foll. = following; folls. = follows; mm. = millimetres; cm. = centimetre(s); in. = inch(es); st.st. = stocking stitch; M = main colour; C = contrast colour.

BACK AND FRONT (alike)

Cast on 104(112:120:128:136) sts. with M using 2¾mm. needles.
Work 9 rows in st.st.; k. 1 row on wrong side to denote hemline.
Change to 3¼mm. needles. Work 10 rows. Join in C. Work 14 rows.
Break C. With M, cont. until work measures 20 cm. (7¾ in.) from hemline, finishing after a p. row. Now inc. 1 st. at both ends of next and every foll. 6th row until there are 118(126:134:142:150) sts.
Cont. until work measures 36 cm. (14 in.) from hemline, finishing after a p. row.

Shape Sleeves
Cast on 16 sts. at beg. of next 10 rows. [278(286:294:302:310) sts.]
Begin sleeve bands:
1st row: with C, k. these 9 sts. with C, k. to end with M. With 2nd ball of C, cast on 9 sts.
2nd row: p., keeping colours as set and twisting yarns when changing colour to avoid leaving holes in the work.
3rd row: Join in 2nd ball of M. Cast on 14 sts. k. 14 M, k.9C, k.278(286:294:302: 310) M, k.9C.
Join in 3rd ball of M.
Cast on 14 sts. [324(332:340:348:356) sts.]
Working colours as set, cont. until sleeve edge measures 12(13:14:15:16) cm. (4¾(5:5½:5¾:6¼) in.), finishing after a p. row.

Shape Upper Sleeves and Shoulders
Cast off 14 sts. with M at beg. of next 2 rows, then 9 sts. with C at beg. of foll. 2 rows.
Cast off 9 sts. with M at beg. of next 10(10:10:12:12) rows. [188(196:204:194:202) sts.]

Work Shoulder Band

Break M. Join in C. Cast off 9 sts. at beg. of next 12 rows and 10(12:16:11:13) at beg. of foll. 2 rows. [60(64:64:64:68) sts.]
Break C. Join in M. Work 9 rows. k. 1 row on wrong side. Change to 2¾mm. needles. Work 9 rows. Cast off very loosely.

MAKING UP

Press on the wrong side under a damp cloth. Sew up upper sleeve, shoulder, neckband, side and underarm seams using the matching yarn for each colour section.
Press seams. Turn in and hem lower edge and neck facing. Double M edge of cuff to wrong side and hem. Press hems.

Traditional Round-neck Sweater

Long-sleeved, hip-length, round neck sweater in very soft wool, with ribbed welts, in stocking stitch

★ Suitable for beginners

MATERIALS

Yarn
Pingouin Pingolaine 4 ply
7(7:8:8) × 50g. balls

Needles
1 pair 3mm.
1 pair 3¼mm.

MEASUREMENTS

Bust
82(87:92:97) cm.
32(34:36:38) in.

Length
54(55:56:57) cm.
21¼(21½:22:22¼) in.

Sleeve Seam
45(45:46:46) cm.
17¾(17¾:18:18) in.

TENSION

28 sts. and 36 rows = 10 cm. (4 in.) square over stocking stitch on 3¼mm. needles. If your tension square does not correspond to these measurements, adjust the needle size used.

ABBREVIATIONS

k.=knit; p.=purl; st(s).=stitch(es); inc.= increase; dec.=decrease; beg.=begin(ning); rem. = remain(ing); rep. = repeat; alt. = alternate; tog. = together; sl. = slip stitch (transfer one stitch from left needle, knitwise unless otherwise stated, to right hand needle.); cont. = continue; patt. = pattern; foll. = following; folls. = follows; mm. = millimetres; cm. = centimetre(s); in. = inch(es); st.st. = stocking stitch.

BACK

** Cast on 109(117:125:133) sts. with 3mm. needles.
1st row: k.2, * p.1, k.1, rep. from * to last st., k.1.
2nd row: k.1, * p.1, k.1, rep. from * to end.
Rep. these 2 rows until work measures 6 cm. (2¼ in.) ending with 2nd row.
Change to 3¼mm. needles and st.st.
Beg. with a k. row, work 8 rows in st.st.
Now dec. 1 st. at both ends of next and every foll. 6th row 5 times in all.
Cont. on rem. 99(107:115:123) sts. until work measures 19 cm. (7½ in.), including rib. Now inc. 1 st. at both ends of next and every foll. 6th row until there are 117(125:133:141) sts.

Cont. without shaping until work measures 36 cm. (14 in.) from beg., ending with p. row.

Armhole Shaping
Cast off 4 sts. at beg. of next 2 rows, 2 sts. at beg. of next 2(2:4:4) rows and 1 st. at beg. of next 4(8:6:10) rows. **
Cont. on rem. 101(105:111:115) sts. until armholes measure 18(19:20:22) cm. (7(7½:7¾:8½) in.), ending with a p. row.

Shoulder and Neck Shaping
Cast off 8(8:9:9) sts. at beg. of next 4 rows.
5th row: cast off 8(8:9:9) sts., k. until there are 17(19:18:20) sts. on right needle, cast off next 19(19:21:21) sts., k. to end. Finish this left side first. [25(27:27:29) sts.]
Cast off 8(8:9:9) sts. at beg. of next row.
Cast off 10 sts. at beg. of foll. row, k. to end. Cast off rem. 7(9:8:10) sts.
Rejoin yarn to neck edge of rem. sts., having wrong side facing.
Cast off 10 sts., p. to end.
Cast off rem. 7(9:8:10) sts.

FRONT

Work as for back from ** to **
Cont. on rem. 101(105:111:115) sts. until armholes measure 12(13:14:14) cm. (4¾(5:5½:5½) in.), ending with a p. row.

Neck Shaping
k. 42(44:46:48) sts. and leave on holder or spare needle, cast off next 17(17:19:19) sts., k. to end.
Cont. on rem. 42(44:46:48) sts. for right front.
Work 1 row straight.
* Now cast off 3 sts. at beg. of next row, 2 sts. at beg. of foll. 3 alt. rows, and 1 st. on foll. 2 alt. rows. [31(33:35:37) sts.]
Cont. straight until armhole matches back armhole in length, ending at armhole edge.

Shoulder Shaping
Cast off 8(8:9:9) sts. at beg. of next and 2 foll. alt. rows.
Work 1 row.
Cast off rem. 7(9:8:10) sts. *
With wrong side facing rejoin yarn to neck edge of left front sts.
Work as for right front from * to *.

SLEEVES

Cast on 59(61:63:65) sts. with 3mm. needles.
Work 1st and 2nd rows of back until work measures 6 cm. (2¼ in.) ending with a 2nd row.
Change to 3¼mm. needles, and work in st.st., beg. with a k. row, inc. 1 st. at both

ends of every 6th row until there are 93(97:101:105) sts.
Cont. straight until work measures 45(45:46:46) cm. (17¾(17¾:18:18) in.) from beg.

Shape Top
Cast off 4 sts. at beg. of next 2 rows, 2 sts. at beg. of next 6(8:8:10) rows, 1 st. at beg. of next 30(30:32:32) rows, 2 sts. at beg. of next 10 rows and 3 sts. at beg. of next 2 rows.
Cast off rem. 17(17:19:19) sts.

NECKBAND

Sew right shoulder seam.
With right side of work facing, using 3mm. needles pick up and knit 67(73:79:85) sts. round front neck edge and 46(46:48:48) sts. across back neck.
Beg. with 2nd row work in rib, as for back, for 11 rows.
Cast off loosely ribwise.

MAKING UP

Sew left shoulder and neckband seam.
Sew in sleeves.
Sew up side and sleeve seams.
Press st.st. fabric and seams very lightly with warm iron and damp cloth.

Soft, Shoulder-fastened Blouse

Simple blouse in furry yarn with ribbed welts and yoke, main body in elongated garter stitch, fastened with bobbles at shoulders

★ Suitable for beginners

MATERIALS

Yarn
Pingouin Oued
4(4:5) × 50g. balls

Needles
1 pair 2¾mm.
1 pair 3¼mm.

Buttons
4

MEASUREMENTS

Bust
82(87:92) cm.
32(34:36) in.

Length
47(48:48) cm.
18½(18¾:18¾) in.

Sleeve Seam
44 cm.
17¼ in.

TENSION

20 sts. and 15 rows = 9 cm. (3½ in.) square over pattern on 3¼mm. needles. If your tension square does not correspond to these measurements, adjust the needle size used.

ABBREVIATIONS

k.=knit; p.=purl; st(s).=stitch(es); inc.= increase; dec.=decrease; beg.=begin(ning); rem. = remain(ing); rep. = repeat; alt. = alternate; tog. = together; sl. = slip stitch (transfer one stitch from left needle, knit-wise unless otherwise stated, to right hand needle.); cont. = continue; patt. = pattern; foll. = following; folls. = follows; mm. = millimetres; cm. = centimetre(s); in. = inch(es); m.1 = pick up horizontal loop lying before next st. and work into back of it.

BACK

Cast on 97(103:109) sts. with 2¾mm. needles.
1st row: k.1, * p.1, k.1, rep. from * to end.
2nd row: p.1, * k.1, p.1, rep. from * to end.

Rep. last 2 rows until work measures 6 cm. (2¼ in.) at centre from start, ending with 2nd row and dec. 1 st. at end of last row. [96(102:108) sts.]
Change to 3¼mm. needles and patt. as folls.:
1st row: right side facing, k. into front and back of each st. all along.
2nd row: * k.1, drop next st. off needle, rep. from * to end.

These 2 rows form patt. Cont. in patt. until work measures 27 cm. (10½ in.) at centre from start, ending with 2nd row.

Shape Armholes
Cast off 4 sts. at beg. of next 2 rows, 3 sts. at beg. of next 4 rows, then dec. 1 st. at each end of every row until 72(74:76) sts. rem.
Next row: k.8(7:8) sts., m.1, * k.2, m.1, rep. from * to last 8(7:8) sts., k.8(7:8) sts. [101(105:107) sts.]
Starting with 1st row, change to k.1, p.1 rib as for welt, and shape yoke by inc. 1 st. at each end of every foll. 10th row until there are 107(111:113) sts., taking inc. sts. into rib.
Work straight in rib until work measures 44(46:46) cm. (17¼(18:18) in.) at centre from start, ending with the right side facing.

Shape Shoulders
Cast off in rib 3 sts. at beg. of next 16 rows. Cast off rem. 59(63:65) sts. in rib.

FRONT

Work as for back.

SLEEVES

Cast on 51(55:55) sts. with 2¾mm. needles and work 6 cm. (2¼ in.) k.1, p.1 rib as for main part, ending with 1st row.
Next row: rib 3(5:5) sts., m.1, * rib 9, m.1, rep. from * to last 3(5:5) sts., rib 3(5:5) sts. [57(61:61) sts.]
Change to 3¼mm. needles.
1st row: work in patt. as for main part, shaping sides by inc. 1 st. at each end of 4th and every foll. 8th row until there are 71(75:75) sts., taking inc. sts. into patt.
Work a few rows straight until sleeve seam measures 44 cm. (17¼ in.), ending with right side facing.

Shape Top
Cast off 4 sts. at beg. of next 2 rows., 3 sts. at beg. of next 6 rows., then 2 sts. at beg. of every row until 21 sts. rem. (all sizes). Cast off.

MAKING UP

Press lightly on wrong side, omitting rib-bing and taking care not to spoil the patt. Join shoulder, side and sleeve seams; in-sert sleeves. Sew a button on each side of front and back, 2 cm. (¾ in.) from end of shoulder. Make a double loop with remaining yarn and join the 2 buttons together with it to form a shoulder fasten-ing as illustrated. Finish rem. pair of but-tons in the same way.
Press all seams.

'Sampler' Slipover Waistcoat

Sleeveless slipover with moss, diagonal, striped rib, garter and oblique stitch bands, and separating bar between each

★ Suitable for beginners

MATERIALS

Yarn
Rowan Classic Tweed DK
5(5:6) × 50g. hanks

Needles
1 pair 3¼mm.
1 pair 5mm.
1 set of double pointed, or one circular needle 3¼mm.

MEASUREMENTS

Bust
87(92:97) cm.
34(36:38) in.

Length
57.5 cm.
22½ in.

TENSION

20 sts. and 32 rows = 10 cm. (4 in.) square over garter stitch on 5mm. needles. If your tension square does not correspond to these measurements, adjust the needle size used.

ABBREVIATIONS

k.=knit; p.=purl; st(s).=stitch(es); inc.= increase; dec.=decrease; beg.=begin(ning); rem. = remain(ing); rep. = repeat; alt. = alternate; tog. = together; sl. = slip stitch (transfer one stitch from left needle, knitwise unless otherwise stated, to right hand needle.); cont. = continue; patt. = pattern; foll. = following; folls. = follows; mm. = millimetres; cm. = centimetre(s); in. = inch(es); p.s.s.o.= pass slipped stitch over; m.st. = moss stitch; g.st. = garter stitch.

BACK

**Cast on 92(100:108) sts. with 3¼mm. needles.
Work in k.1, p.1 rib for 8 cm. (3¼ in.)
Change to 5mm. needles.
Work 6 rows raised separating bar patt.:
1st row (right side), *4th and 5th rows*: k.
2nd, 3rd and 6th rows: p.
Work m. st. band:
1st row: k.1, p.1, rep. to end.
2nd row: p.1, k.1, rep. to end.
Cont. until band measures 8cm. (3¼ in.), ending with a wrong side row.

Now work 6 rows raised separating bar patt.
Work diagonal st. band:
1st row: k.2, p.2, rep. to end.
2nd, 4th, 6th and 8th rows: k. all k. sts., p. all p. sts.
3rd row: k.1, * p.2, k.2, rep. from * to last 3 sts., p.2, k.1.
5th row: p.2, k.2 to end.
7th row: p.1, * k.2, p.2, rep. from * to last 3 sts., k.2, p.1.
Cont. until band measures 8 cm. (3¼ in.), ending with a wrong side row.
Now work 6 row raised separating bar patt.
Work g.st. band:
k. every row until band measures 8 cm. (3¼ in.) deep, ending with a wrong side row.
Now work 6 row raised separating bar patt.
Work striped ribbing band and armhole:
1st row: cast off 5(6:7) sts., (k.1, p.1) to end.
2nd row: cast off 5(6:7) sts., p. to end.
3rd row: cast off 5(6:7) sts., (p.1, k.1) to end.
4th row: as 2nd row. [72(76:80) sts.]
5th row: k.1, p.1 to end.
6th row: p. **
Rep. 5th and 6th rows until the band measures 8 cm. (3¼ in.).
Now work 6 row raised separating bar patt.
Work oblique stitch band and shoulder shaping:
1st row: k.3, p.1, rep. to end.
2nd, 4th, 6th and 8th rows: k. all the k. sts., p. all the p. sts.
3rd row: p.1, k.3, rep. to end.
5th row: k.1, p.1, k.2, rep. to end.
7th row: p.2, p.1, k.1, rep. to end.
Rep. these 8 rows once more, then rows 1 and 2.*
Keeping patt. correct, cast off 4 (5:6) sts. at beg. of next 4 rows.
Cast off 4 sts. at beg. of next 6 rows. [32 sts.]
Cast off rem. sts. loosely.

FRONT

Work as for back from ** to **.
Rep. rows 5 and 6 of striped ribbing band once more, then row 5 again.
Next row: p. 28(30:32) sts., cast off 16 sts., p. to end.
Finish this side first:
1st row: k.1, p.1 to end.
2nd row: dec. 1 st., p. to end.
Rep. these 2 rows 7 times more. [20(22:24) sts.]

Now work 6 row raised separating bar patt., dec. 1 st. at neck edge on 2nd and 4th rows.
Work oblique st. patt. from * to * as back.
** Cast off 4(5:6) sts. at beg. of next and foll. alt. row.
Work 1 row.
Cast off 4 sts. twice, 2 sts. once on next and foll. 2 alt. rows.
Fasten off. **
Finish right side:
Rejoin yarn.
1st row: k.1, sl.1, p.s.s.o., * k.1, p.1 rep. from, * to end.
2nd row: p.
Rep. these 2 rows 7 times more. [20(22:24) sts.]
Now work 6 row raised separating bar patt., dec. 1 st. at neck edge on 2nd and 4th rows.
Work oblique st. patt. from * to * as back.
Work 1 row.
Work as for other side of front from ** to **.

NECKBAND

Sew shoulder seams using backstitch to create a gently sloping shoulder. Starting at right-hand end of back neck, using set of double pointed or circular 3¼mm. needles, pick up and knit 32 sts. across back neck, 50 sts. down left side of opening, 16 sts. across cast off lower section of neck opening, and 50 sts. up right side of opening. [148 sts.]
Work 8 rows of g.st. Cast off loosely.
Now pick up and knit 70 sts. evenly around armhole edge, beg. at armhole edge.
Work 8 rows of g.st. Cast off loosely.

MAKING UP

Sew up side seams including bands. Press lightly with damp cloth and warm iron.

Rib-and-twist stitch Sweater

1948

Crew-neck sweater in stocking stitch with twisted rib panels, set-in sleeves and ribbed welts

★★ Suitable for knitters with some previous experience

MATERIALS

Yarn
Patons Clansman 4 ply
8(8:9:9:10) × 50g. balls

Needles
1 pair 2¾mm.
1 pair 3¼mm.

MEASUREMENTS

Chest
92(97:102:107:112) cm.
36(38:40:42:44) in.

Length
65(66:66:67:67) cm.
25½(26:26:26¼:26¼) in.

Sleeve Seam
46(46:47:47:47) cm.
18(18:18½:18½:18½) in.

TENSION

28 sts. and 36 rows = 10 cm. (4 in.) square over st. st. on 3¼mm. needles. If your tension square does not correspond to these measurements, adjust the needle size used.

ABBREVIATIONS

k. = knit; p. = purl; st(s). = stitch(es); inc. = increase; dec. = decrease; beg. = begin(ning); begin(ning); rem. = remain(ing); rep. = repeat; alt. = alternate; tog. = together; sl. = slip (transfer one stitch from left needle, knitwise unless otherwise stated, to right hand needle.); cont. = continue; patt. = pattern; foll. = following; folls. = follows; mm. = millimetres; cm. = centimetres; in. = inches; st. st. = stocking st.: one row k., one row p.; g. st. = garter st.: every row k.; incs. = increases; decs. = decreases; m.1 = make 1 st.: pick up horizontal loop lying before next st. and work into back of it; Tw.2R = k. into front of 2nd st. on left needle, then k. into front of first st. on left needle and sl. both sts. off needle tog.; Tw.2L = k. into back of 2nd st. on left needle, then k. into front of first st. on left needle and sl. both sts. off needle tog.

BACK

** Cast on 119(127:135:143:151) sts. with 2¾mm. needles.
1st row (right side): k.1, * p.1, k.1, rep. from * to end.
2nd row: p.1, * k.1, p.1, rep. from * to end.
Rep. last 2 rows until work measures 7 cm. (2¾ in.), ending with a 1st row.
Next row: p.3(7:3:7:4), m.1, (p.3(6:4:8:5), m.1) 3(1:3:1:3) times, p.3(6:4:8:4), * k.1, (p.1, k.1) 4 times, p.3(2:5:4:5), m.1,

(p.4(3:4:3:5), m.1) 1(2:1:2:1) times, p.4(3:4:3:5), rep. from * 3 times, k.1, (p.1, k.1) 4 times, p.3(7:3:7:4), m.1, (p.3(6:4: 8:5), m.1) 3(1:3:1:3) times, p.3(6:4:8:4). [135(143:151:159:167) sts.]
Change to 3¼mm. needles and work in patt. as folls.:
1st row (right side): k.19(21:23:25:27), * p.1, (k.1, p.1) 4 times, k.13(14:15:16:17), rep. from * 3 times, p.1, (k.1, p.1) 4 times, k.19(21:23:25:27).
2nd row: p.19(21:23:25:27), * k.1, (p.1, k.1) 4 times, p.13(14:15:16:17), rep. from * 3 times, k.1, (p.1, k.1) 4 times, p.19(21:23: 25:27).
3rd-8th rows: as 1st and 2nd 3 times.
9th row: k.17(19:21:23:25), Tw.2R, * p.1, (k.1, p.1) 4 times, Tw.2L, k.9(10:11:12:13), Tw.2R, rep. from * 3 times, p.1, (k.1, p.1) 4 times, Tw.2L, k.17(19:21:23:25).
10th row: as 2nd.
11th row: k.21(23:25:27:29), * p.1, (k.1, p.1) twice, k.17(18:19:20:21), rep. from * 3 times, p.1, (k.1, p.1) twice, k.21(23:25: 27:29).
12th row: p.21(23:25:27:29), * k.1, (p.1, k.1) twice, p.17(18:19:20:21), rep. from * 3 times, k.1, (p.1, k.1) twice, p.21(23:25: 27:29).
13th-20th rows: as 11th and 12th 4 times.
21st row: k.19(21:23:25:27), Tw.2R, * p.1, (k.1, p.1) twice, Tw.2L, k.13(14:15:16:17), Tw.2R, rep. from * 3 times, p.1, (k.1, p.1) twice, Tw.2L, k.19(21:23:25:27).
22nd row: as 12th.
These 22 rows form patt.
Work straight in patt. until back measures 43 cm. (16¾ in.) from beg., ending with a wrong side row.

Shape Armholes
Keeping patt. straight, cast off 4 sts. at beg. of next 2 rows, then dec. 1 st. at each end of next and every foll. alt. row until 103(107:111:115:119) sts. rem. **
Work straight until back measures 65(66:66:67:67) cm. (25½(26:26:26¼:26¼) in.) from beg., ending with a wrong side row.

Shape Shoulders
Cast off 11(10:11:12:11) sts. at beg. of next 2 rows.
Cast off 10(11:11:11:12) sts. at beg. of next 4 rows.
Leave rem. 41(43:45:47:49) sts. on a spare needle.

FRONT

Work as for back from ** to **.
Work straight until front measures 57(58:
58:59:59) cm. (22¼(22¾:22¾:23¼:23¼)
in.) from beg., ending with a wrong side
row.

Divide for Neck

Next row: patt. 39(40:41:42:43), turn and
leave rem. sts. on a spare needle.
Cont. on these 39(40:41:42:43) sts. for first
side.
Dec. 1 st. at neck edge on next and every
alt. row until 31(32:33:34:35) sts. rem.
Work straight until front matches back to
shoulder, ending with a wrong side row.

Shape Shoulder

Cast off 11(10:11:12:11) sts. at beg. of next
row.
Cast off 10(11:11:11:12) sts. at beg. of foll.
2 alt. rows.
With right side facing, sl. centre 25(27:29:
31:33) sts. on a spare needle.
Rejoin yarn to rem. sts., patt. to end.
Complete to match first side.

SLEEVES

Cast on 63(67:67:71:71) sts. with 2¾mm.
needles.

Work 7 cm. (2¾ in.) in k.1, p.1 rib as for
back, ending with a 1st row.
Next row: p.3(4:4:3:3), (m.1, p.2(5:5:3:3)
2(1:1:2:2) times, * k.1, (p.1, k.1) 4 times,
p.3(2:2:5:5), (m.1, p.4(3:3:4:4)) 2(3:3:2:2)
times, rep. from * once, k.1, (p.1, k.1) 4
times, p.3(4:4:3:3), (m.1, p.2(5:5:3:3))
2(1:1:2:2) times. [71(75:75:79:79) sts.].
Change to 3¼mm. needles and patt.
1st row (right side): k.9(10:10:11:11), * p.1,
(k.1, p.1) 4 times, k.13(14:14:15:15), rep.
from * once, p.1, (k.1, p.1) 4 times,
k.9(10:10:11:11).
2nd row: p.9(10:10:11:11), * k.1, (p.1, k.1) 4
times, p.13(14:14:15:15), rep. from * once,
k.1, (p.1, k.1) 4 times, p.9(10:10:11:11).
These 2 rows set patt.
Cont. in patt. to match back, shaping
sides by inc. 1 st. at each end of 11th and
every foll. 8th row until there are
99(103:103:107:107) sts., taking inc. sts.
into st. st.
Cont. straight until sleeve seam measures
46(46:47:47:47) cm. (18(18:18½:18½:18½)
in.), ending with a wrong side row.

Shape Top

Working in patt., cast off 4 sts. at beg. of
next 2 rows.

Now dec. 1 st. at each end of next and
every alt. row until 51 sts. rem.
Work 1 row straight, then dec. 1 st. at
each end of every row until 27 sts. rem.
Cast off.

Neck Border

Sew up right shoulder seam.
With right side facing and 2¾mm.
needles, beg. on left front shoulder, pick
up and k.31 sts. down left side of neck,
k.25(27:29:31:33) from centre, pick up
and k.31 sts. up right side, then k.41
(43:45:47:49) from back. [128(132:136:140:
144) sts.]
Work 7 rows in k.1, p.1 rib.
Cast off evenly in rib.

MAKING UP

Press work lightly on wrong side, omit-
ting welt, cuff and neck ribbing, taking
care not to spoil patt.
Sew up left shoulder seam, then sew up
neck border with a flat seam.
Sew up side and sleeve seams.
Set in sleeves.
Press all seams.

Cashmere, Self-stripe Sweater

Very long, slim, boat-neck, cashmere sweater in textured rib pattern,
with drop shoulders, buttoned cuffs and placket on lower edge

---

★★ Suitable for knitters with some
previous experience

MATERIALS

Yarn

Yarn Store Cashmere
360(380)g.
Also available in kit form including buttons by mail order, see page 168.

Needles

1 pair 3mm.
1 pair 3¼mm.
1 circular 3mm.

Buttons

14 shirt-size (included in kit)

MEASUREMENTS

Bust

82–87(92–97) cm.
32–34(36–38) in.

Length

69(72) cm.
27(28¼) in.

Sleeve Seam

38(39) cm.
15(15¼) in.

TENSION

36 sts. and 40 rows = 10 cm. (4 in.) square
over patt. on 3¼mm. needles. If your tension square does not correspond to these
measurements, adjust the needle size
used.

ABBREVIATIONS

k.=knit; p.=purl; st(s).=stitch(es); inc.=
increase; dec.=decrease; beg.=begin(ning);
rem. = remain(ing); rep. = repeat; alt. =
alternate; tog. = together; sl. = slip stitch
(transfer one stitch from left needle, knit-

---

wise unless otherwise stated, to right
hand needle.); cont. = continue; patt. =
pattern; foll. = following; folls. = follows;
mm. = millimetres; cm. = centimetres; in.
= inch(es); st.st. = stocking stitch; m.1 =
make 1 st.: pick up horizontal loop lying
before next st., and k. into back of it; y.r.n.
= yarn round needle.

BACK

Cast on 189(201) sts. with 3mm. needles,
and work in rib as folls.:
1st row: p.1, sl.1, (k.1, p.1) 5 times, k.1, *
sl.1, k.1, p.1, k.1, rep. from * to last 10 sts.,
(p.1, k.1) 4 times, sl.1, p.1.
2nd row: k.1, k. all k. sts. and p. all p. sts.,
ending k.1.
Rep. rows 1 and 2 until 50 rows have been
worked, ending on wrong side.
51st row: cast off 11 sts., patt. to last 11 sts.,
cast off. Break yarn, leaving enough for
sewing up. [169(179) sts.]

52nd row: k.1, p. to last st., k.1.
Change to 3¾mm. needles and work in patt. as folls.:
1st row: p.1, * sl.1, k.3, rep. from * ending last rep. sl.1, p.1.
2nd row: k.1, p. to last st., k.1.
Rep. patt. until work measures 46(48) cm. (18(18¾) in.) from cast-on edge, ending on wrong side.

Shape Armholes
Keeping continuity of patt., work as folls.:
1st row: p.1, m.1, * sl.1, k.3, rep. from *, ending last rep. sl.1, m.1, p.1.
2nd row: k.1, m.1, p. to last st., m.1, k.1.
3rd row: p.1, k.2, * sl.1, k.3, rep. from *, ending last rep. sl.1, k.2, p.1.
4th row: as 2nd row.
5th row: p.1, m.1, k.2, * sl.1, k.3, rep. from *, ending last rep. k.2, m.1, p.1.
6th row: k.1, p. to last st., k.1.
Rep. 1st to 6th rows until 16 sts. have been inc. on each edge. [199(211) sts.]
Work straight for 60(64) rows, ending on wrong side.

Shape Neck
Keeping continuity of patt. work as folls.:

k.59(63) sts., turn and leave rem. sts. on a spare needle.
Cast off 4 sts., then dec. 1 st. at neck edge on every row until 50(54) sts. rem.
Work 1 row.
Cast off.
Leave centre 81(85) sts. on a holder.
With right side facing, rejoin yarn to rem. 59(63) sts., at centre edge.
Work to match first side.

FRONT
Cast on 167(179) sts. with 3mm. needles, and work in rib as folls.:
Rows 1, 3, 7, 9, 11, 13, 17, 19, 21, 23, 27, 29, 31, 33, 37, 39, 41, 43, 47, 49 and 51: p.1, sl.1, (k.1, p.1) 5 times, k.1, * sl.1, k.1, p.1, k.1, rep. from * to last 10 sts., (p.1, k.1) 4 times, sl.1, p.1.
2nd and alt. rows: k.1, k. all k. sts. and p. all p. sts., ending with k.1.
Rows 5, 15, 25, 35 and 45: p.1, sl.1, k.1, p.1, k.1, y.r.n., k.2 tog., (p.1, k.1) 3 times, * sl.1, k.1, p.1, k.1, rep. from * to last 10 sts., (p.1, k.1) twice, y.r.n., k.2 tog., p.1, k.1, sl.1, p.1.
Change to 3¾mm. needles and work in same way as for back, until work measures 46(48) cm. (18(18¾) in.) from cast-on edge, ending on wrong side.

Shape Armhole
Keeping continuity of patt., work armhole shaping as for back.
Work straight for 42(46) rows, ending on wrong side.

Shape Neck
Keeping continuity of patt., work as folls.:
k.83(88) sts., turn and leave rem. sts. on a spare needle.
Cast off 8 sts., then cast off 4 sts. at beg. of foll. 3 alt. rows.
Now dec. 1 st. at neck edge on every row until 50(54) sts. rem.
Work 4 rows.
Cast off.
Leave centre 33(35) sts. on holder.
With right side facing, rejoin yarn to rem. 83(88) sts. at centre edge.
Work to match 1st side.

SLEEVES
Cast on 79(83) sts. with 3mm. needles and work in rib as folls.:

Left Cuff
1st row: p.1, (sl.1, k.1, p.1, k.1) 4 times, sl.1, (k.1, p.1) 5 times, k.1, * sl.1, k.1, p.1, k.1, rep. from *, ending last rep. with sl.1, p.1.
2nd row: k.1, k. all k. sts. and p. all p. sts., ending with k.1.

Right Cuff
1st row: p.1, (sl.1, k.1, p.1, k.1) 12(13) times, [49(53) sts.], sl.1, (k.1, p.1) 5 times, k.1, (sl.1, k.1, p.1, k.1) 4 times, ending last rep. with sl.1, p.1.
2nd row: k.1, k. all k. sts., and p. all p. sts., ending with k.1.

Both Cuffs
Rep. 1st and 2nd rows until work measures 5 cm. (2 in.), ending on wrong side.

Change to 3¾mm. needles and work in patt. as for back.
Inc. 1 st. at each end of 1st and every foll. 6th row 24(25) times, until there are 127(133) sts.
Patt. straight until work measures 38(39) cm. (15(15¼) in.) from cast-on edge.
Cast off.

NECK RIB
Omitting ribbing, press lightly on wrong side.
Sew up shoulder seams, carefully matching patt.
With 3mm. circular needle and right side facing, k. across centre 81(85) sts. on back neck, then pick up and k.67(68) sts. down left side of neck, 33(35) sts. across centre front neck and 67(68) sts. up right side of neck. [248(256) sts.]
Work neck in rib as on back.
Check that the patt. sequence is in line with patt. on centre back and centre front.
Cont. in circular work until neck rib measures 3 cm. (1 in.).
Cast off.

MAKING UP
Insert sleeves by sewing cast-off edge of sleeve to straight edge of armhole.
Sew sleeve seams and side seams using p. sts. on right side edges for seam.
Sew button extension flaps on back rib to underside of front rib.
Press seams.
Sew 5 buttons onto each back extension and 2 buttons onto each sleeve cuff.

Diamond-patterned Twin Set

Cardigan and short-sleeved sweater with contrast bands, neck and hem welts, diamond pattern on sweater front, cardigan hem

★★★ Suitable for experienced knitters

MATERIALS

Yarn
Sunbeam 2 ply
Cardigan and sweater:
15(16:16:17) × 25g. hanks Main Col. A
3(3:4:4) × 25g. hanks Contrast Col. B

Needles
1 pair 3mm.
1 pair 3¾mm.

Buttons
9

MEASUREMENTS

Bust (both)
87(92:97:102) cm.
34(36:38:40) in.

Length (both)
66(67:67:69) cm.
26(26½:26½:27) in.

Sleeve Seam (sweater)
11·5 cm.
4½ in.

Sleeve Seam (cardigan)
42(43:43:44) cm.
16½(16¾:16¾:17¼) in.

TENSION

26 sts. and 34 rows = 10 cm. (4 in.) square over stocking stitch on 3¾mm. needles. If your tension square does not correspond to these measurements, adjust the needle size used.

ABBREVIATIONS

k.=knit; p.=purl; st(s).=stitch(es); inc.= increase; dec.=decrease; beg.=begin(ning); rem. = remain(ing); rep. = repeat; alt. = alternate; tog. = together; sl. = slip stitch (transfer one stitch from left needle, knitwise unless otherwise stated, to right hand needle.); cont. = continue; patt. = pattern; foll. = following; folls. = follows; mm. = millimetres; cm. = centimetres; in. = inch(es); st.st. = stocking stitch.

SWEATER BACK

Cast on 121(127:133:139) sts. with 3mm. needles and A.
Work 6 cm. (2 in.) in k.1, p.1 rib.
Change to 3¾mm. needles and st.st.
Cont. straight until work measures 42(43:43:44) cm. (16½(16¾:16¾:17¼) in.).

Shape Armholes
Cast off 8(9:9:10) sts. at beg. of next 2 rows.
Dec. 1 st. at each end of next 6 rows, then dec. 1 st. at each end of every alt. row until 89(93:99:103) sts. rem.
Cont. straight until work measures 62(63:63:65) cm. (24¼(24¾:24¾:25½) in.)

Shape Shoulders
Cast off 9(10:10:11) sts. at beg. of next 4 rows.

Cast off 10(10:11:11) sts. at beg. of next 2 rows.
Cast off rem. 33(33:37:37) sts.

SWEATER FRONT

Work as back until work measures 52(53·5:53·5:55) cm. (20½(21:21:21½) in.).
Now work from Chart A.
[Note: Chart shows half of design. To complete the row follow chart across from right to left, beg. at point marked for size being worked then omitting centre st., follow chart back across same row to beg. Always twist yarns when changing colours to prevent holes.]
Work until you have completed row 26.
27th row: now, keeping pattern correct throughout, work 32(34:35:37) sts., work 2 tog., turn.
28th row: work 2 tog., work to end of row.
29th – 32nd rows: work 4 more rows, dec. 1 st. at neck edge on each row.
33rd row: cast off 9(10:10:11) sts., work to end.
34th row: work to end.
Using A only, cast off 9(10:10:11) sts., work to end. Work one row.
Next row: cast off rem. sts.
Return to sts. on needle and slip centre 21(21:25:25) sts. onto pin holder for neck.
Rejoin wool to rem. 34(36:37:39) sts. and work in patt., starting at point marked B for size you are making, working between markers, work row 27 from left to right, 28 from right to left, etc.
Next row: work 2 tog., work to end of row. Work 5 more rows, dec. 1 st. at neck edge on each row.

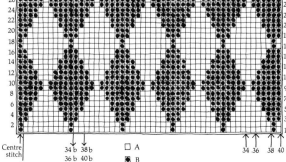

Chart A

Centre stitch
a
34 b 38 b
36 b 40 b
□ A
◼ B
34 36 38 40

Work 1 row.
Cast off 9(10:10:11) sts. at beg. of next 2 alt.
rows.
Work 1 row.
Cast off rem. sts.

SWEATER SLEEVES

Cast on 78(80:82:84) sts. with 3mm.
needles and A.
Work in k.1, p.1 rib for 2·5 cm. (1 in.).
Change to 3¾mm. needles and st.st. and
inc. 1 st. at each end of 5th and then every
6th row until there are 86(88:90:92) sts.
Cont. straight until work measures 11 cm.
(4½ in.).

Shape Top

Cast off 8(9:9:10) sts. at beg. of next 2 rows.
Work 2 tog. at each end of every alt. row
until 36 sts. rem.
Cast off 3 sts. at beg. of next 4 rows.
Cast off rem. sts.
Finishing: sew right shoulder seam.

NECKBAND

With B and 3mm. needles and with right
side of work facing, pick up and knit
89(93:93:97) sts. including sts. on holder.
Work in k.1, p.1 rib for 5 cm. (2 in.).
Cast off very loosely in rib. Sew up rem.
shoulder seam.
Turn down and stitch neckband.

CARDIGAN BACK

Cast on 121(127:135:141) sts. with 3mm.
needles and work 5 cm. (2 in.) in k.1, p.1
rib.
Change to 3¾mm. needles and st.st.
Work Chart B from bottom to top, working
each row from right to left beg. at size marker and back from point B to size marker
on the right, as before.
With A only, cont. straight until work
measures 43(44:44:45) cm. (16¾(17¼:
17¼:17¾) in.).

Shape Armholes

Cast off 8(9:9:10) sts. at beg. of next 2 rows.
Dec. 1 st. at each end of next 6 rows, then
dec. 1 st. at each end of every alt. row until
89(93:101:105) sts. rem.
Cont. straight until work measures
65(66:66:67) cm. (25½(26:26:26¼) in.).
Cast off 9(10:10:11) sts. at beg. of next 4
rows.
Cast off 10(10:11:11) sts. at beg. of next 2
rows.
Cast off rem. sts.

CARDIGAN LEFT FRONT

Cast on 71(75:77:81) sts. with 3mm.
needles and B and work 5 cm. (2 in.) in
k.1, p.1 rib. Change to 3¾mm. needles,
and st.st. Now follow Chart C, starting at
size marker and working left to right on
1st row, right to left on 2nd row etc. On 1st
row work across 60(64:66:70) patt. sts.
Place 11 sts. left after working across patt.
sts. on a holder for front band, to be worked later.
Cont. working to top of Chart C.
With A only, cont. straight until work
measures 43(44:44:45) cm. (16¾(17¼:

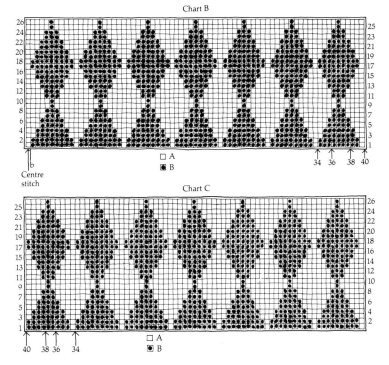

Chart B

□ A
◉ B
b
Centre
stitch

34 36 38 40

Chart C

40 38 36   34

□ A
◉ B

17¼:17¾) in.), finishing at side edge.
Cast off 8(9:9:10) sts. at beg. of next row.
Work one row.
Dec. 1 st. at armhole edge on next 6 rows.
Then dec. 1 st. at armhole edge of next 2
alt. rows. [44(47:49:52) sts.]
Now work straight until work measures
60(61:61:62) cm. (23½(24:24:24¼) in.)
finishing at neck edge.
Next row: work next 8(9:9:10) sts. and place
these on a holder, work to end of row.
Now dec. 1 st. at neck edge on next
2(2:3:3) rows, then at neck edge of every
alt. row until 28(30:31:33) sts. rem.
Cont. straight until work measures same
as back to shoulder shaping, finishing at
armhole edge.
Cast off 9(10:10:11) sts. at beg. of next 2 alt.
rows.
Cast off rem. 10(10:11:11) sts.

Buttonband

Place the 11 sts. from holder on 3mm.
needles and with B work in k.1, p.1 rib
until band is long enough to fit along front
edge when very slightly stretched.
Place sts. on holder. Mark position of 9
buttons placing first one 1 cm. (½ in.) from
lower edge and allowing for last one to be
in the centre of the 2 cm. (1 in.) neckband,
which is worked later.

CARDIGAN RIGHT FRONT

Work as for left front reversing shapings
and chart and working buttonholes to correspond to position of buttons on button-
band each worked as folls.:
Work 4 sts., cast off 3 sts., work 3 sts.

Next row: work across row, casting on 3
sts. over cast off sts.

CARDIGAN SLEEVES

Cast on 64(66:70:72) sts. with 3mm.
needles using A and work 6 cm. (2¼ in.)
in k.1, p.1 rib.
Change to 3¾mm. needles and st.st. and
inc. 1 st. at each end of 5th and every foll.
6th row until there are 76(82:86:90) sts.
Then inc. 1 st. at each end of every 8th row
until there are 94(96:98:100) sts.
Cont. straight until work measures
42(43:43:44) cm. (16½(16¾:16¾:17¼) in.).

Shape Top

Cast off 8(9:9:10) sts. at beg. of next 2 rows.
Work 2 sts. tog. at each end of every alt.
row until 40 sts. rem.
Cast off 3 sts. at beg. of next 6 rows.
Cast off rem. sts.

CARDIGAN NECKBAND

With B and 3mm. needles and with right
side of work facing, pick up and
k.113(115:117:119) sts. around neck edge
including sts. on holder from bands.
Work in k.1, p.1 rib for 5 cm. (2 in.),
remembering to make a buttonhole twice
on both front and back of neckband,
which is later folded over.
Cast off very loosely in rib and turn down
neckband and stitch.

MAKING UP

Sew seams.
Set in sleeves.
Sew bands in place.

Moss-stitch, Crew-neck Sweater 1981

Hip-length, nubbly sweater in moss stitch, with roomy crew neckline, set-in sleeves and ribbed welts

★ Suitable for beginners

MATERIALS

Yarn
Sunbeam Aran Tweed
13(14:15) × 50g. balls

Needles
1 pair 5mm.
1 pair 6mm.

MEASUREMENTS

Bust
82(87:92) cm.
32(34:36) in.

Length
59(59:60) cm.
23¼(23¼:23½) in.

Sleeve Seam
46 cm.
18 in.

TENSION

8 sts. and 12 rows = 5 cm. (2 in.) square over moss stitch on 6mm. needles. If your tension square does not correspond to these measurements, adjust the needle size used.

ABBREVIATIONS

k.=knit; p.=purl; st(s).=stitch(es); inc.= increase; dec.=decrease; beg.=begin(ning); rem. = remain(ing); rep. = repeat; alt. = alternate; tog. = together; sl. = slip stitch (transfer one stitch from left needle, knit-wise unless otherwise stated, to right hand needle.); cont. = continue; patt. = pattern; foll. = following; folls. = follows; mm. = millimetres; cm. = centimetres; in. = inch(es); st.st. = stocking stitch.

BACK

Cast on 63(65:67) sts. with 5mm. needles.
1st row: k.1, * p.1, k.1, rep. from * to end.
2nd row: p.1, * k.1, p.1, rep. from * to end.
Rep. these 2 rows until work measures 10 cm. (4 in.), ending with a 1st row.
Next row: p., inc. 6(8:10) sts. evenly across row. [69(73:77) sts.]
Change to 6mm. needles and cont. in moss st. as folls.:
1st row (right side): k.1, * p.1, k.1, rep. from * to end.
2nd row: as 1st row.
These 2 rows form the patt.

Cont. in moss st. until work measures 40 cm. (15¾ in.) from beg., ending with 2nd row (right side facing).

Shape Armhole
Cont. in moss st. and at the same time cast off 4 sts. at beg. of next 2 rows, then dec. 1 st. at both ends of next and foll. 6(7:8) alt. rows. [49(51:53) sts.]
Work straight in moss st. until back measures 59(59:60) cm. (23¼(23¼:23½) in.) from beg.
Cast off.

FRONT

Work as for back until front measures 51(51:52) cm. (20(20:20½) in.) from beg., ending with right side facing for next row.

Shape Neck
Cont. in moss st., patt. 17(18:19) sts. and leave these sts. (right front) on spare needle or holder. Cast off 15 sts., patt. to end.
Cont. patt. on these 17(18:19) sts. for left front.
1st row: patt. to last 2 sts., dec. 1 st.
2nd row: patt.

Rep. these 2 rows twice more. [14(15:16) sts.]
Work straight in moss st. until front measures 59(59:60) cm. (23¼(23¼:23½) in.).
Cast off.
Rejoin wool at neck edge of right front and cont. in patt., dec. on neck edge as folls.:
1st row: dec. 1 st., patt. to end.
2nd row: patt.
Rep. these 2 rows twice more. [14(15:16) sts.]
Complete to match left front.

SLEEVES

Cast on 37(39:41) sts. with 5mm. needles.
1st row: k.1, * p.1, k.1, rep. from * to end.
2nd row: p.1, * k.1, p.1, rep. from * to end.
Rep. these 2 rows until work measures 10 cm. (4 in.), ending with 1st row.
Next row (with wrong side facing): p., inc. 1 st. at both ends of row. [39(41:43) sts.]
Change to 6mm. needles and cont. in moss st. as front, inc. 1 st. at both ends of every 10th row 3 times. [45(47:49) sts.]
Work straight in moss st. until sleeve seam measures 46 cm. (18 in.) from beg. ending with right side facing.

Shape Top
Cast off 4 sts. at beg. of next 2 rows, then dec. 1 st. at both ends of next and every alt. row until 11 sts. rem.
Cast off.

NECKBAND

Sew up right shoulder seam, backstitching cast-off sts. on right shoulder with equivalent number on back cast-off edge. With right side of work facing, using 5mm. needles, pick up and k.18 sts. down left front neck shaping, 15 sts. across centre front neck, 18 sts. up right front neck shaping and 31 sts. across back neck. [82 sts.]
Cont. in rib.
1st row: k.1, p.1, to end of row.
2nd row: p.1, k.1, to end of row.
Rep. these rows once more.
Cast off loosely in rib.

MAKING UP

Join left shoulder seam, and invisibly join ribbing on neckband. Sew in sleeves, gathering any fullness at top of sleeve into shoulder. Sew up side and sleeve seams. Press all seams lightly on wrong side with a warm iron and damp cloth.

V-neck Golfing Cardigan

Stocking-stitch cardigan with knitted horizontal check line, crochet vertical line, hemmed cuffs and lower edge and set-in sleeves

★★ Suitable for knitters with some previous experience

MATERIALS

Yarn
Patons Clansman DK
9(10:11) × 50g. balls Main Col. A
2(2:2) × 50g. balls Contrast Col. B

Needles
1 pair 3¼mm.
1 pair 3¾mm.
1 3mm. crochet hook

Buttons
6 leather

MEASUREMENTS

Bust
87(92:97) cm.
34(36:38) in.

Length
54(58:64) cm.
21¼(22¾:25) in.

Sleeve Seam
42 cm.
16½ in.

TENSION

24 sts. and 34 rows = 10 cm. (4 in.) square over patt. on 3¾mm. needles. If your tension square does not correspond to these measurements, adjust the needle size used.

ABBREVIATIONS

k.=knit; p.=purl; st(s).=stitch(es); inc.= increase; dec.=decrease; beg.=begin(ning); rem. = remain(ing); rep. = repeat; rep(s). = repeat(s); alt. = alternate; tog. = together; sl. = slip stitch (transfer one stitch from left needle, knitwise unless otherwise stated, to right hand needle.); cont. = continue; patt. = pattern; foll. = following; folls. = follows; mm. = millimetres; cm. = centimetres; in. = inch(es); st.st. = stocking stitch.

BACK

Cast on 112(123:134) sts. with 3¼mm. needles and A.
Starting with a k. row, work 7 rows in st.st.

Next row: k. into back of each st. to end to form hemline ridge.
Change to 3¾mm. needles and work in patt., joining in and breaking off colours as required. **
1st row (right side): k.6, * p.1, k.10, rep. from * to last 7 sts., p.1, k.6.
2nd row: p.6, * k.1, p.10, rep. from * to last 7 sts., k.1, p.6.
3rd to 12th row: as 1st and 2nd row, 5 times.
13th row: in B, as 1st.

14th row: in A, as 2nd.
These 14 rows form patt.
Work a further 7(8:9) patt. reps. ***

Shape Armholes

Keeping patt. correct, cast off 7 sts. at beg. of next 2 rows, then 4 sts. at beg. of foll. 2 rows.
Now dec. 1 st. at each end of next and every alt. row until 84(95:106) sts. rem.
Cont. in patt. until armhole measures 18(19:20) cm. (7(7½:7¾) in.), ending with a wrong side row.

Shape Neck

Next row: patt. 29(33:37), turn and leave rem. sts. on spare needle.
Dec. 1 st. at neck edge on every row until 25(29:33) sts. rem.
Work straight until armhole measures 20(21:22) cm. (7¾(8¼:8½) in.), ending with a wrong side row.
Cast off.
With right side facing, rejoin appropriate yarn to rem. sts.
Cast off centre 26(29:32) sts., work to end. Work to match first side, reversing shapings.

RIGHT FRONT

Cast on 57(62:68) sts. with 3¼mm. needles and A, and work as back to ***, noting that patt. on 2nd size will read:
1st row: * p.1, k.10, rep. from * to last 7 sts., p.1, k.6.
2nd row: p.6, * k.1, p.10, rep. from * to last st., k.1.

Shape Armhole and Neck

Work as folls., keeping patt. correct throughout:
Next row: k.2 tog., patt. to end.
Cast off 7 sts. at beg. of next row.
Work 1 row.
Next row: cast off 4 sts., work to last 2 sts., dec. 1 st.
Now dec. 1 st. at armhole edge on next and foll. 2 alt. rows, at the same time dec. 1 st. at front edge on every foll. 3rd row from previous dec. until 40(45:51) sts. rem.
Now dec. 1 st. on every 3rd row at front edge only until 25(29:33) sts. rem.
Work straight until front matches back at armhole edge, ending with a wrong side row.
Cast off.

LEFT FRONT

Work as for right front, reversing shapings and reversing patt. for 2nd size.

SLEEVES

Cast on 57(68:79) sts. with 3¼mm. needles and A and work as for back to **. Now work in patt. as on back, shaping sides by inc. 1 st. at each end of 7th and every foll. 9th row until there are 81(92:103) sts., taking inc. sts. into patt. Work straight until 10 patt. reps. in all have been completed.

Shape Armholes

Cast off 7 sts. at beg. of next 2 rows, then dec. 1 st. at each end of next and every alt. row until 23(24:25) sts. rem.
Work 1 row.
Cast off 4 sts. at beg. of next 2 rows.
Cast off rem. sts.

FRONT BAND

Cast on 14 sts. with 3¼mm. needles and A and work 8 rows in k.1, p.1 rib.
1st buttonhole row: rib 6, cast off 2 sts., rib to end.
2nd buttonhole row: rib, casting on 2 sts. over those cast off on previous row.
Work 16 rows in k.1, p.1 rib.
Work a further buttonhole as before.
Cont. thus until 6(7:8) buttonholes in all have been worked.
Now work in rib until band fits from ridge up right front, round back of neck and down left front to ridge, when very slightly stretched.
Cast off in rib.

MAKING UP

Omitting ribbing, press lightly on wrong side following instructions on the ball band.
With 3mm. crochet hook and B, work a chain up each p. row on right side to complete the black squares.
Sew up shoulder seams.
Insert sleeves.
Sew up side and sleeve seams, matching patt.
Fold hem at ridge to wrong side and sl.-hem loosely in position.
Sew on front band.
Press seams.
Sew on buttons.

Fine-knit Classic Sweater

Loose, hip-length, round-neck, unisex sweater in stocking stitch, with ribbed hem, cuffs and doubled-over neckband

★ Suitable for beginners

MATERIALS

Yarn
Sirdar Country Style 4 ply
6(7:8:8:9:10:10) × 50g. balls

Needles
1 pair 2¾mm.
1 pair 3¼mm.
2 stitch holders

MEASUREMENTS

Bust/Chest
82(87:92:97:102:107:112) cm.
32(34:36:38:40:42:44) in.

Length
54(55:56:60:61:62:64) cm.
21¼(21½:22:23½:24:24¼:25) in.

Sleeve Seam
42(43:45:46:47:49:49) cm.
16½(16¾:17¾:18:18½:19¼:19¼) in.

TENSION

14 sts. and 18 rows = 5 cm. (2 in.) square over patt. on 3¼mm. needles. If your tension square does not correspond to these measurements, adjust the needle size used.

ABBREVIATIONS

k.=knit; p.=purl; st(s).=stitch(es); inc.= increase; dec.=decrease; beg.=begin(ning); rem. = remain(ing); rep. = repeat; alt. = alternate; tog. = together; sl. = slip stitch (transfer one stitch from left needle, knit-wise unless otherwise stated, to right hand needle.); cont. = continue; patt. = pattern; foll. = following; folls. = follows; mm. = millimetres; cm. = centimetres; in. = inch(es); st.st. = stocking stitch; m.1 = make 1 st.: pick up horizontal loop lying before next st. and k. or p. into back of it.

BACK

Cast on 113(121:127:135:141:149:155) sts. with 2¾mm. needles.
Work in k.1, p.1 rib for 8 cm. (3¼ in), inc. on last row as folls.:
Rib 6(10:14:8:11:10:13), m.1, (rib 10(10:10: 12:12:13:13), m.1) 10 times, rib 7(11:13:7: 10:9:12). [124(132:138:146:152:160:166) sts.]
Change to 3¼mm. needles and, starting with a k. row, work in st.st.

Cont. straight until work measures 36(36:36:37:37:37:37) cm. (14(14:14:14½: 14½:14½:14½) in.) from beg.

Shape Armholes
Cast off 6(7:8:8:8:9:9) sts. at beg. of next 2 rows.
Dec. 1 st. at both ends of the next 3 rows.
Dec. 1 st. at both ends of the foll. 8(9:9:7:8: 9:10)alt. rows. [90(94:98:110:114:118:122) sts.]
Work straight until armhole measures 18(19:21:23:24:26:27) cm. (7(7½:8¼:9:9½: 10¼:10½) in.)

Shape Shoulders
Cast off 5(5:5:7:7:7:7) sts. at beg. of next 8 rows, and 5(6:7:4:5:6:7) sts. at beg. of next 2 rows.
Leave rem. 40(42:44:46:48:50:52) sts. on a holder.

FRONT

Work as given for back until armhole measures 13(14:15:18:19:21:22) cm. (5(5½: 5¾:7:7½:8¼:8½) in.

Shape Neck
K.33(34:35:40:41:42:43) sts., turn, leave rem. sts. on a spare needle.
* Dec. 1 st. at neck edge on the next and foll. 7 alt. rows. [25(26:27:32:33:34:35) sts.]
Work straight until length matches back to shoulder, ending at side edge.

Shape Shoulder
Cast off 5(5:5:7:7:7:7) sts. at beg. of next and foll. 3 alt. rows.
Work 1 row.
Cast off 5(6:7:4:5:6:7) sts.
Return to rem. sts., right side facing.
Sl. the next 24(26:28:30:32:34:36) sts. onto a holder, rejoin yarn to next st. and k. to end of row.
Complete to match first side from * to end.

SLEEVES

Cast on 51(55:59:63:67:71:75) sts. with 2¾mm. needles.
Work in k.1, p.1 rib for 8 cm. (3 in.), inc. 1 st. on the last row. [52(56:60:64:68:72: 76) sts.]
Change to 3¼mm. needles and, starting with a k. row, work in st.st.
Inc. 1 st. at both ends of the next and every foll. 6th row until there are 92(96:100:106:110:114:118) sts.
Work straight until sleeve measures 42(43:45:46:47:49:49) cm. (16½(16¾:17¼: 18:18½:19¼:19¼) in.)

Shape Top
Cast off 6(7:8:8:8:9:9) sts. at beg. of next 2 rows.
Dec. 1 st. at both sides of the next 3 rows.
Dec. 1 st. at both ends of every foll. alt. row until there are 42(42:42:42:44:44:46) sts. Work 1 row.
Cast off 4 sts. at beg. of next 8 rows.
Cast off rem. 10(10:10:10:12:12:14) sts.

NECKBAND

Sew up left shoulder seam.
With 2¾mm. needles, and right side facing, pick up and k.40(42:44:46:48:50:52) sts. from back neck, 24 sts. from left side front neck, 24(26:28:30:32:34:36) sts. from centre front neck, and 24 sts. from right side front neck. [112(116:120:124: 128:132:136) sts.]
Work in k.1, p.1 rib for 5 cm. (2 in.).
Cast off fairly loosely in rib.

MAKING UP

Press work on the wrong side under a damp cloth, omitting ribbing.
Sew up right shoulder and neckband.
Fold neckband onto wrong side and sew down.
Set in sleeves, matching centre of sleeve head to shoulder seam.
Sew up side and sleeve seams.

Tailored, Plaid Sports Cardigan

Round-neck cardigan in stocking stitch, shaped at the waistline,
with plaid pattern worked from chart, on fronts only, and additional
swiss darning

★★★ Suitable for experienced knitters only

MATERIALS

Yarn
Lister-Lee Motoravia 4 ply
6(6:7) × 50g. balls Colour A (beige)
1 × 50g. ball Colour B (green)
1 × 50g. ball Colour C (rust)

Needles
1 pair 2¾mm.
1 pair 3mm.

MEASUREMENTS

Bust
82(87:92) cm.
32(34:36) in.

Length
56 cm.
21 in.

Sleeve Seam
46 cm.
18 in.

TENSION

14 sts. and 18 rows = 5 cm. (2 in.) square on 3mm. needles. If your tension square does not correspond to these measurements, adjust the needle size used.

ABBREVIATIONS

k.=knit; p.=purl; st(s).=stitch(es); inc.= increase; dec.=decrease; beg.=begin(ning); rem. = remain(ing); rep. = repeat; alt. = alternate; tog. = together; sl. = slip stitch (transfer one stitch from left needle, knit-wise unless otherwise stated, to right hand needle.); cont. = continue; patt(s). = pattern(s); foll. = following; folls. = follows; mm. = millimetres; cm. = centi-metre(s); in. = inch(es); st.st. = stocking stitch.

LEFT FRONT

Cast on 65(69:73) sts. using 2¾ mm. needles.
1st row: * k.1, p.2, k.1, rep. from * to last 9 sts., k.9.
2nd row: p.9, * p.1, k.2, p.1, rep. from * to end.
Rep. 1st and 2nd rows 4 times more.
Using 3mm. needles, beg. patt. and side shaping, working in st.st.:
1st row: k.2 tog., k.14(16:18) work 1st row of graph over next 39 sts., knit to end.

Keeping edge sts. in Colour A, cont. to work the 39 sts., from chart (39 rows) until 5 complete patts. have been worked, noting that each alt. rep. will beg. on a purl row (i.e. 1st patt. starts on a knit row, 2nd patt. starts on a purl row), then work remainder of front all in Colour A, at the same time, work shapings as follows: dec. 1 st. at side edge on every 3rd row until 52(56:60) sts. rem.
Cont. without shaping until work measures 18 cm. (7 in.). Now inc. one st. at side edge on next and every foll. 5th row until there are 65(69:73) sts.
Cont. without shaping until work measures 38 cm. (15 in.), ending at inc. edge.

Shape Armhole

Cast off 4(5:6) sts. at beg. of next row. Work one row.
Cast off 3(4:5) sts. at beg. of next row. Work one row.
Cast off 3 sts. at beg. of next row. Work one row.
Cast off 2 sts. at beg. of next row.
Dec. 1 st. at armhole edge on next 2 rows. [51(53:55) sts.] Cont. in patt. until armhole measures 15½ cm. (6 in.), ending at arm-hole edge.

Shape Neck

1st row: patt. to last 8 sts., leave these 8 sts. on a thread for neckband.
Cast off 4 sts. at beg. of next row. Work one row.
(Cast off 3 sts. at beg. of next row. Work one row) twice.
Cast off 1(2:3) sts. at beg. of next row. Work one row.
Cast off 1 st. at beg. of next and foll. alt. row. [30(31:32) sts.]

Shape Shoulder

Cast off 5(6:7) sts. at beg. of next row. Work one row.
Cast off 5 sts. at beg. of next and foll. 4 alt. rows.
Work embroidered stitches from chart.

RIGHT FRONT

Work to correspond with left front, revers-ing all shapings and working 5 button-holes as folls.:
1st buttonhole row (9th row of rib): k.2, cast off 4 sts., k.2, rib to end.
Next row: cast on 4 sts. over cast off sts.
Work 2nd buttonhole on 39th row of 1st patt., thus – purl to last 6 sts., cast off 4 sts., p.2. Cast on 4 sts. over cast off sts. on next row.

Work 3rd buttonhole on 39th row of 2nd patt., 4th buttonhole on 39th row of 3rd patt. and 5th buttonhole on 39th row of 4th patt.

BACK

Worked in Colour A throughout.
Cast on 116(124:132) sts. using 2¾mm. needles.

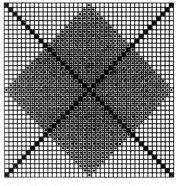

□ A ◨ B ☒ C: worked in swiss darning.

1st row: * k.1, p.2, k.1, rep. from * to end.
2nd row: * p.1, k.2, p.1, rep. from * to end.
Rep. 1st and 2nd rows 4 times more.
Using 3mm. needles, cont. in st.st., dec. 1 st. at each end of first and every foll. 3rd row until 90(98:106) sts. rem. Cont. in st. st. until work measures 18 cm. (7 in.). Inc. 1 st. at each end of next and every following 5th row until there are 116(124:132) sts. Cont. without shaping until work measures same as left front to armhole.

Shape Armholes
Cast off 3(4:5) sts. at beg. of next 2 rows.
Cast off 3 sts. at beg. of next 2 rows.
Cast off 1(2:3) sts. at beg. of next 2 rows.
Dec. 1 st. at each end of next 4 rows.
[94(98:102)sts.] Cont. without shaping until work measures same as left front to shoulder.

Shape Shoulders
Cast off 5(6:7) sts. at beg. of next 2 rows.
Cast off 5 sts. at beg. of next 10 rows.
Leave rem. 34(36:38) sts. on a thread for neckband.

SLEEVES
Worked in Colour A throughout.
Cast on 58(60:62) sts. using 2¾mm. needles and work 7 cm. (2¾ in.) in k.2, p.2 rib as given for back.
Using 3mm. needles, cont. in st.st., inc. 1 st. at each end of first and every foll. 8th row until there are 96(98:100) sts.
Cont. without shaping until work measures 46 cm. (18 in.) or desired length of sleeve seam, ending with a wrong side row.

Shape Head
Cast off 4 sts. at beg. of next 2 rows.
Cast off 3 sts. at beg. of next 2 rows.
Cast off 2 sts. at beg. of next 2 rows. Dec. 1 st. at beg. of next and every foll. row until 58 sts. rem.
Dec. 1 st. at each end of every foll. 4th row until 50 sts. rem.
Cast off 4 sts. at beg. of next 4 rows.
Cast off 5 sts. at beg. of next 2 rows.
Cast off rem. 22(24:26) sts.

NECKBAND
Sew shoulder seams. Using 2¾mm. needles and Colour A, slip the 8 sts. from right front onto needles, pick up and knit 28(29:30) sts. to shoulder seam, knit across 34(36:38) sts. of back, pick up and knit 28(29:30) sts. down left front, knit across 8 sts. on thread. [106(110:114) sts.]
1st row: p.8, * k.2, p.2, rep. from * to last 10 sts., k.2, p.8. Work 4 more rows in k.2, p.2 rib with foll. 8 sts. in st.st. Work a buttonhole on next 2 rows. Work 4 more rows and cast off.

MAKING UP
Press as instructions on ball band. Sew up side and sleeve seams. Sew in sleeves. Work one row double crochet in Colour A around edges of front bands. Face with ribbon if required (make buttonholes in ribbon to correspond with knitted buttonholes, and buttonhole st. both together). Sew on buttons to correspond with buttonholes.

Classic Mohair Cardigan   1965

Simple, hip-length cardigan with long sleeves, hemmed lower edge and wide neck welt

★ Suitable for beginners

MATERIALS

Yarn
Emu Filigree
10(11:11:12:12) × 25g. balls

Needles
1 pair 5mm.
1 pair 5½mm.

Buttons
5

Facing Ribbon
1½ metres (1¾ yards)

MEASUREMENTS

Bust
82(87:92:97:102) cm.
32(34:36:38:40) in.

Centre Back
61(62:63:64:64) cm.
24(24½:24¾:25¼:25¼) in.

Sleeve Seam
45(46:46:47:47) cm.
17¾(18:18:18½:18½) in.

TENSION

14 sts. and 20 rows = 10 cm. (4 in.) square over st.st. on 5½mm. needles. If your tension square does not correspond to these measurements, adjust the needle size used.

ABBREVIATIONS

k.=knit; p.=purl; st(s).=stitch(es). inc.=increase; dec.=decrease; beg.=begin(ning); rem. = remain(ing); rep. = repeat; alt. = alternate; tog. = together; sl. = slip stitch (transfer one stitch from left needle, knitwise unless otherwise stated, to right hand needle.); cont. = continue; patt. = pattern; foll. = following; folls. = follows;

mm. = millimetres; cm. = centimetres; in. = inch(es); st.st. = stocking stitch.

BACK

Cast on 63(67:71:75:79) sts. loosely with 5mm. needles.
Work in st.st., starting with a p. row, for 6 rows.
Next row: k., using a 5½mm. needle, working into the back of the stitch. Change back to 5mm. needles and work a further 5 rows in st.st., starting with a k. row.
Next row: fold up cast off edge to inside and p. the next st. tog. with 1st st. of cast on edge: work in this manner across row, thus forming the hem.
Change to 5½mm. needles.
Now, starting with a k. row, cont. straight in st.st. until the work measures 40 cm. (15¾ in.) from the cast on edge, ending with a p. row.

Shape Armholes
Cast off 3 sts. at beg. of next 2 rows.
Dec. 1 st. at each end of every foll. alt. row 5(6:7:8:8) times in all. [47(49:51:53:57) sts.]
Cont. in st.st. on these sts. until work measures 20(21:22:23:23) cm. (7¾(8¼:8½: 9:9) in.) from beg. of armhole shaping, ending with a p. row.

Shape Shoulders
Cast off 4(4:5:5:6) sts. at beg. of next 2 rows.
Cast off 5 sts. at beg. of foll. 2 rows.
Cast off 29(31:31:33:35) sts. loosely for back neck.

LEFT FRONT

Cast on 37(39:41:43:45) sts. loosely with 5mm. needles.
Work in st.st, starting with a p. row, for 6 rows.
Next row: k., using a 5½mm. needle, and working into back of st.
Change back to 5mm. needles and cont. in st.st. with rib at centre front edge as folls.:
1st row (right side): k. to last 6 sts., * p.1, k.1, rep. from * to end.
2nd row: * p.1, k.1, rep. from * twice more, p. to end.
Rep. these 2 rows once more, then work the 1st row again.
Next row: work row to fold up hem as given for the back, but working the 1st 6 sts. ribwise.
Change to 5½mm. needles and, starting with a 1st row, work the 2 row patt. as given until work measures 40 cm. (15¾ in.) ending with a 2nd row, at the armhole edge.

Shape Armholes
Cast off 5 sts. at beg. of next row, work to end.
Work 1 row.
Dec. 1 st. at beg. of next and every foll. alt. row, 4(5:6:7:8) times in all. [28(29:30:31:32) sts.]
Cont. in patt. on these sts. until work measures 15(16:17:18:18) cm. (6(6¼:6½:

7:7) in.) from beg. of armhole shaping, ending at armhole edge.

Shape Neckline
Next row: work in patt. to last 13 sts., place these 13 sts. on safety pin, turn.
Work 1 row.
Dec. 1 st. at neck edge of next 6(7:7:8:8) rows.
Cont. in st.st. until work measures 20(21:22:23:23) cm. (7¾(8¼:8½:9:9) in.) from beg. of armhole shaping, ending at armhole edge.

Shape Shoulders
Cast off 4(4:5:5:6) sts. at beg. of next row.
Work 1 row.
Cast off rem. 5 sts.
Mark position of buttons as folls.: the 1st is 9 cm. (3½ in.) from hemline edge, the last is 7·5 cm. (3 in.) below centre front neck point (the 5th buttonhole is on the neckline), the rem. 2 are evenly spaced between these 2.

RIGHT FRONT

Work as given for the left front, reversing shapings, and working buttonholes to correspond to markings on left front.

Work each buttonhole as folls.:
1st row: cast off the 2 centre sts. of the 6 st. rib section.
2nd row: cast on 2 sts. over those cast off on previous row.

SLEEVES

Cast on 35(37:39:41:43) sts. with 5mm. needles.
Work in single rib as folls.:
1st row: k.2, * p.1, k.1, rep. from * to last st., k.1.
2nd row: k.1, * p.1, k.1, rep. from * to end.
Rep. these 2 rows until work measures 5 cm. (2 in.), ending with a 2nd row.
Change to 5½mm. needles and cont. in st.st., inc. 1 st. at each end of every foll. 8th row until there are 51(53:55:57:59) sts., then cont. without shaping until work measures 45(46:46:47:47) cm. 17¾(18:18: 18½:18½) in.) from cast on edge, ending with a p. row.

Shape Top Sleeve
Cast off 4 sts. at beg. of next 2 rows.
Dec. 1 st. at each end of every foll. alt. row, 8 times.
Dec. 1 st. at each end of every row, 4(5:6:7:8) times in all.
Cast off 5 sts. at beg. of next 3 rows.
Cast off rem. 4 sts.

COLLAR

Using small backstitch, sew up both shoulder seams.
Using 5½mm. needles, and working from the right side, pick up 13 sts. from safety pin at righthand front edge, 13(15:17: 17:19) sts. from back neck, 13(15: 17:17:19) sts. from neck edge and rem. 13 sts. from safety pin. [83(89:95:95:101) sts.]
1st row (wrong side): p.1 * k.1, p.1, rep. from * to end.
2nd row: k.1, * p.1, k.1, rep. from * to end.
Rep. these 2 rows until 12 rows have been worked.
AT THE SAME TIME make buttonhole above previous buttonholes, on the 6th and 7th rows.
When 12 rows have been worked, mark this row with a thread, then change to 5mm. needles and work a further 13 rows, making a buttonhole, as before, on the 6th and 7th rows of this section.
Cast off loosely in rib.

MAKING UP

Sew collar to inside, and hem down loosely.
Neatly oversew two sides of buttonhole on collar together.
Sew sleeve seams and side seams, using small backstitch.
Pin sleeves into place and sew.
Sew facing ribbon to front edges.
Make buttonholes in ribbon and oversew edges of them.
Sew buttons into place.

Round-neck Stripey Sweater

Two-tone sweater with three-quarter length set-in sleeves, garter stitch welts and round neck with ribbed border

★ Suitable for adventurous beginners

MATERIALS

Yarn
Sirdar Country Style 4 ply
3(3:3:4) × 50g. balls (Main Colour)
3(3:3:3) × 50g. balls (Contrast Colour)

Needles
1 pair 2¾mm.
1 pair 3¼mm.
2 stitch holders

MEASUREMENTS

Bust
82(87:92:97) cm.
32(34:36:38) in.

Length
55(56:57:58) cm.
22(22½:22¾:23¼) in.

Sleeve Seam
33 cm. (approx)
13¼ in. (approx.)

TENSION

14 sts. and 20 rows = 5 cm. (2 in.) square over stocking stitch on 3¼mm. needles. If your tension square does not correspond to these measurements, adjust the needle size used.

ABBREVIATIONS

k.=knit; p.=purl; st(s).=stitch(es); inc.= increase; dec.=decrease; beg.=begin(ning); rem. = remain(ing); rep. = repeat; alt. = alternate; tog. = together; sl. = slip stitch (transfer one stitch from left needle, knit-wise unless otherwise stated, to right hand needle.); cont. = continue; patt. = pattern; foll. = following; folls. = follows; mm. = millimetres; cm. = centimetre(s); in. = inch(es); st.st. = stocking st; g.st. = garter st; M = main colour; C = contrast colour.

BACK

Cast on 104(112:120:128) sts. using M, with 2¾mm. needles. Work 6 rows in g.st. Change to 3¼mm. needles and patt. of 6 rows st.st. in C, 6 rows st.st. in M. Cont. until work measures 18 cm. (7 in.). Inc. at both ends of next and every foll. 6th row until there are 118(126:134:142) sts. Cont. until work measures 37 cm. (14½ in.), ending after a p.row.

Shape Armholes
Cast off 4 sts. at beg. of next 2 rows, then dec. 1 st. at both ends of every row until 90(94:98:102) sts. rem.
Cont. until work measures 17(18:19:20) cm. (6½(7:7½:7¾) in.) from beg. of arm-holes, ending after a k. row.

Shape Neck and Shoulders
Next row: p.55(57:59:61) sts., place the last 20 sts. worked on a holder, p. to end. Cont. on last set of sts. worked for right side. Cast off 7(7:8:8) sts. at beg. of next side edge row and 3 sts. at beg. of next neck edge row. Rep. these 2 rows twice more. Cast off rem. 5(7:6:8) sts. **
Join yarn to inner edge of rem. sts. and work to end. Work from ** to **.

FRONT

Work as back until work measures 12(13:14:15) cm. (4¾(5:5½:5¾) in.) from beg. of armholes, finishing after a k. row.

Shape Neck
Next row: p.52(54:56:58) sts., place the last 14 sts. worked on a holder, p. to end. Cont. on last set of sts. worked for left side.
*** Dec. at neck edge on every row until 26(28:30:32) sts. rem. Cont. until work matches back to outer shoulder.

Shape Shoulders
Cast off 7(7:8:8) sts. at beg. of next 3 side edge rows. Work to side edge. Cast off rem. 5(7:6:8) sts. ***
Join yarn to outer edge of rem. sts. Work from *** to ***.

SLEEVES

Cast on 52(56:60:64) sts. using M, with 2¾mm. needles. Work 6 rows in g.st. Change to 3¼mm. needles and patt. as for main part. Inc. 1 st. at both ends of next and every foll. 6th row until there are 88(92:96:100) sts. Cont. until work measures approx. 33 cm. (13 in.), finishing after the same row of patt. as back and front before beg. armhole shaping.

Shape Top
Cast off 4 sts. at beg. of next 2 rows. Dec. at both ends of next and every alt. row until 44 sts. rem.; p.1 row.
Dec. at both ends of every row until 28 sts. rem. Cast off 3 sts. at beg. of next 4 rows. Cast off rem. 16 sts.

NECKBAND

With right side of work facing, using C and 2¾mm. needles, k. up 10 sts. along 1st side of back neck, k. central 20 sts., k. up 10 sts. along 2nd side. Work 6 rows in k.1, p.1 rib. Change to M. Work a further 6 rows in k.1, p.1 rib. Cast off in rib.
With right side of work facing, using C and 2¾mm. needles, k. up 30 sts. along 1st side of front neck, k. central 14 sts., and k. up 30 sts. along 2nd side. Complete as back neckband.

MAKING UP

Press work on the wrong side under a damp cloth, omitting g.st. and ribbing. Sew up side, shoulder, neckband and sleeve seams. Set sleeves into armholes. Press seams.

Sweater with Garter-stitch Insert 1954

Simple, unisex, thick sweater with V-shaped garter-stitch front 'insert',
set-in sleeves and ribbed welts

★ Suitable for beginners

MATERIALS

Yarn
Lister-Lee Motoravia DK
9(9:10:11:11:12) × 50g. balls

Needles
1 pair 3¼mm.
1 pair 4mm.

MEASUREMENTS

Bust/Chest
82(87:92:97:102:107) cm.
32(34:36:38:40:42) in.

Length
54(57:60:62:65:67) cm.
21¼(22¼:23½:24¼:25½:26¼) in.

Sleeve Seam
49(49:49:52:52:52) cm.
19¼(19¼:19¼:20½:20½:20½) in.

TENSION

22 sts. and 28 rows = 10 cm. (4 in.) square
over st.st. on 4mm. needles. If your tension square does not correspond to these
measurements, adjust the needle size
used.

ABBREVIATIONS

k.=knit; p.=purl; st(s).=stitch(es); inc.=
increase; dec.=decrease; beg.=begin(ning);
rem. = remain(ing); rep. = repeat; alt. =
alternate; tog. = together; sl. = slip stitch
(transfer one stitch from left needle, knit-
wise unless otherwise stated, to right
hand needle.); cont. = continue; patt. =
pattern; foll. = following; folls. = follows;
mm. = millimetres; cm. = centimetres; in.
=. inch(es); st.st. = stocking stitch; g.st.

= garter stitch: all rows k.; m.1 = make 1
st.: pick up horizontal loop lying before
next st. and work into back of it.

BACK

Cast on 87(91:97:103:109:113) sts. with
3¼mm. needles.
1st row: k.1, * p.1, k.1, rep. from * to end.
2nd row: p.1, * k.1, p.1, rep. from * to end.
Rep. 1st and 2nd rows for 10 cm. (4 in.)
ending with 1st row.
Next row: k.1, m.1, rib 5(2:5:5:4:6), m.1, *
rib 15(12:12:13:14:11), m.1, rep. from * to
last 6(4:7:6:6:7) sts., rib to end. [94(100:
106:112:118:124) sts.]
Change to 4mm. needles.
Cont. in st.st. until work measures
36(38:41:42:44:46) cm. (14(15:16:16½:17¼:
18) in.), ending with a p. row.

Shape Armholes
Cast off 5 sts. at beg. of next 2 rows.
Dec. 1 st. at each end of next and foll. alt.
rows 5(6:7:7:8:10) times. [74(78:82:88:
92:94) sts.]
Cont. straight until work measures
54(57:60:62:65:67) cm. (21¼(22¼:23½:
24½:25½:26¼) in.], ending with a p. row.

Shape Shoulders
Cast off 7(8:8:9:9:9) sts. at beg. of next 4
rows.
Cast off 7(7:8:9:10:10) sts. at beg. of next 2
rows.
Leave rem. 32(32:34:34:36:38) sts. on
holder.

FRONT

Work as back until front measures 18 cm.
(7 in.), ending with a k. row.

Work Insert
1st row: p.46(49:52:55:58:61), k.2, p. to
end.
2nd and every alt. row: k.
3rd row: rep. 1st row.
5th row: p.45(48:51:54:57:60), k.4, p. to
end.
7th row: rep. 5th row.
9th row: p.44(47:50:53:56:59), k.6, p. to
end.
Cont. to work 1 more st. each side of g.st.
panel every 4th row to end of work.
AT THE SAME TIME, shape armholes as
for the back, until work measures 48(51:
54:55:58:60) cm. (18¾(20:21¼:21½:22¾:
23½) in.) from beg. ending with a
p. row.

Shape Neck
Next row: patt. 30(32:33:36:37:37) sts., turn
work and leave rem. sts. on spare needle.

Dec. 1 st. at neck edge on every row 5
times.
Dec. 1 st. at neck edge on alt. rows 4 times.
[21(23:24:27:28:28) sts.]
Cont. straight, shaping shoulder as on
back.
Return to sts. on spare needle.
Sl. 14(14:16:16:18:20) sts. onto a holder.
Rejoin yarn and work to match first side,
reversing all shapings.

SLEEVES

Cast on 41(43:45:49:51:53) sts. with
3¼mm. needles.
Work in k.1, p.1 rib for 9 cm. (3½ in.),
ending with a 1st row.
Next row: rib 2(3:4:6:3:4), m.1, * rib
4(4:4:4:5:5), m.1, rep. from * to last
3(4:5:7:3:4) sts., rib to end. [51(53:55:59:
61:63) sts.]
Change to 4mm. needles.
Cont. in st.st.
AT THE SAME TIME, inc. 1 st. at each end
of 3rd and every foll. 8th row. [73(75:77:
81:83:85) sts.]
Cont. straight until work measures
49(49:49:52:52:52) cm. (19¼(19¼:19¼:
20½:20½:20½) in.), ending with a p. row.

Shape Top
Cast off 5 sts. at beg. of next 2 rows.
Dec. 1 st. at each end of next and every
foll. alt. row 13(14:15:16:17:18) times.
[37(37:37:39:39:39) sts.]
Cast off 6 sts. at beg. of next 4 rows.
Cast off rem. 13(13:13:15:15:15) sts.

NECKBAND

Sew up right shoulder seam.
With 3¼mm. needles and right side
facing, pick up and k.17(18:19:21:21:21)
sts. down left front neck,
k.14(14:16:16:18:20) from front holder,
pick up and k.17(18:19:21:21:21) up
right front neck, k.15(15:16:16:17:18) sts.
from back holder, k.2 sts. tog., k. rem.
15(15:16:16:17:18) sts. from holder.
[79(81:87:91:95:99) sts.]
Work in p.1, k.1 rib for 4 cm. (1½ in.).
Cast off loosely in rib.

MAKING UP

Press each piece following instructions on
ball band and stretching g.st. insert if
required.
Sew up left shoulder seam, including
neckband.
Sew up side seams. Sew up sleeve seams.
Set in sleeves.
Press seams if required.

Fine Wool T-shirt Sweater

Long, slim sweater in stocking stitch, with ribbed welts, collar and buttoned neck placket, and set-in sleeves

★ Suitable for beginners

MATERIALS

Yarn
Rowan Botany 3 ply
9(9:10:11) × 25g. balls

Needles
1 pair 2¼mm.
1 pair 3mm.

Buttons
3

MEASUREMENTS

Bust
82(87:92:97) cm.
32(34:36:38) in.

Length
60(61:62:63) cm.
23½(24:24¼:24¾) in.

Sleeve
44(44:45:45) cm.
17¼(17¼:17¾:17¾) in.

TENSION

16 sts. and 20 rows = 5 cm. (2 in.) square over stocking stitch on 3mm. needles. If your tension square does not correspond to these measurements, adjust the needle size used.

ABBREVIATIONS

k.=knit; p.=purl; st(s).=stitch(es); inc.= increase; dec.=decrease; beg.=begin(ning); rem. = remain(ing); rep. = repeat; alt. = alternate; tog. = together; sl. = slip stitch (transfer one stitch from left needle, knitwise unless otherwise stated, to right hand needle.); cont. = continue; patt. = pattern; foll. = following; folls. = follows; mm. = millimetres; cm. = centimetre(s); in. = inch(es); p.s.s.o. = pass the slipped stitch over; t.b.l. = through back of loops; st.st. = stocking stitch; sl.1k. = slip one stitch knitwise.

BACK

**Cast on 139(147:155:163) sts. with 2¼ mm. needles.
1st row: k.2, * p.1, k.1, rep. from * to the last st., k.1.

2nd row: * k.1, p.1, rep. from * to the last st., k.1.
Rep. 1st and 2nd rows for 8 cm. (3¼ in.), ending with 2nd row.
Change to 3mm. needles and st.st. Work until back measures 39(41:41:42) cm. (15¼(16:16:16½) in.) from beg., ending with a p. row. **

Shape Armholes
Cast off 2(4:5:7) sts. at beg. of next 2 rows.
3rd row: k.3, sl.1k., k.1, p.s.s.o., k. to last 5 sts., k.2 tog., k.3. Work 3 rows.
Cont. to dec. in this way at each end of next row, and then every 4th row until 109(113:117:121) sts. rem. Work 21(21: 21:23) rows.

Shape Shoulders
Cast off at beg. of next and foll. rows, 6(7:8:7) sts. twice, 7(7:7:8) sts. 6 times, and 7(8:8:8) sts. twice.
Cast off 41(41:43:43) rem. sts. for back of neck.

FRONT

Follow instructions for back from ** to **.

Shape Armholes
Cast off 2(4:5:7) sts. at beg. of next 2 rows.
3rd row: k.3, sl.1k., k.1, p.s.s.o., k. to last 5 sts., k.2 tog., k.3.
4th to 6th rows: Work in st.st.
7th row: As 3rd row.

Shape Front Opening
Next row: p.63(65:68:70) sts., cast off 5 sts., p. to end. Cont. on last set of sts. Work 2 rows.
Next row: k.3, sl.1k., k.1, p.s.s.o., k. to end. Cont. to dec. in this way at beg. of every 4th row until 52(54:56:58) sts. rem. Work 5(5:3:5) rows.

Shape Neck
Next row: k. to last 5 sts., cast off these sts. Break yarn. Turn and rejoin yarn at neck edge. Dec. 1 st. at neck edge on the next 7 rows, and then the 4(4:5:5) foll. alt. rows, ending at armhole edge.

Shape Shoulder
Dec. at neck edge of foll. alt. rows twice more, and at the same time cast off 6(7:8:7) sts. at beg. of next row, and 7(7:7:8) sts. at beg. of 3 foll. alt. rows. Work 1 row. Cast off 7(8:8:8) rem. sts.
Rejoin yarn to rem. sts. at opening edge. Work 2 rows.
Next row: k. to last 5 sts., k.2 tog., k.3. Cont. to dec. in this way at end of every 4th row until 52(54:56:58) sts. rem. Work 5(5:3:5) rows.

Shape Neck
Next row: cast off 5 sts., k. to end.
Now complete to match first side, working 1 row more before shaping shoulder.

SLEEVES

Cast on 63(65:67:69) sts. with 2¼mm. needles and work 8 cm. (3¼ in.) in rib as for back.
Change to 3mm. needles and st.st. Work 4 rows.
Inc. 1 st. at each end of next row, and then every 6th row until there are 77(81:91:95) sts., and then every 8th row until there are 97(101:105:109) sts. Work until sleeve measures 44(44:45:45) cm. (17¼(17¼:17¾:17¾) in.) from beg., ending with a p. row.

Shape Top
Cast off 2(4:5:7) sts. at beg. of next 2 rows.
3rd row: k.3, sl.1k., k.1, p.s.s.o., k. to last 5 sts., k.2 tog., k.3.
4th row: p.3, p.2 tog., p. to last 5 sts., p.2 tog. t.b.l., p.3. Rep. 3rd and 4th rows 5(5:4:4) times more.
Next row: as 3rd row.
Next row: p. Rep. last 2 rows until 37 sts. rem., ending with dec. row.

Cont. as folls.:
1st row: p.2 tog., p. to last 2 sts., p.2 tog.
2nd row: k.2 tog., k. to last 2 sts., k.2 tog.
Rep. 1st and 2nd rows once more, and then 1st row once.
Cast off rem. sts.

RIGHT FRONT BAND

With 2¾mm. needles and right side of work facing, knit up 45 sts. down left front opening edge. (9 sts. for 10 rows).
1st row: * k.1, p.1, rep. from * to the last st., k.1.
2nd row: k.2, * p.1, k.1, rep. from * to the last st., k.1. Rep. 1st and 2nd rows 4 times more. Cast off in rib.

LEFT FRONT BAND

With 2¾mm. needles and starting at cast off sts., knit up sts. as left side. Work in rib as left side. Work 4 rows.
Make buttonholes:
Next row: rib 4 sts., cast off 3 sts., (rib 12 sts. including st. on needle, cast off 3 sts.) twice, rib to end.
Next row: rib to end, casting on 3 sts. over those cast off. Work 4 more rows in rib.
Cast off in rib.

COLLAR

Cast on 139(139:145:145) sts. with 2¾mm. needles.
1st row: k.2, * p.1, k.1, rep. from * to the last st., k.1.
2nd row: * k.1, p.1, rep. from * to the last st., k.1. These 2 rows form rib.
3rd row: rib 5 sts., (k.1, p.1, k.1) into next st., rib to last 6 sts., (k.1, p.1, k.1) into next st., rib 5 sts.
Cont. to inc. in this way at each end of every 6th row until there are 163(163:169:169) sts. Work 3 rows. Cast off in rib.

MAKING UP

Press each piece lightly with warm iron and damp cloth. Sew up shoulder, side and sleeve seams.
Sew sleeves into armholes. Sew lower edge of underwrap at back of overwrap.
Sew cast on edge of collar to neck edge with edges of collar matching centre of borders.
Press seams lightly. Sew on buttons.

Ribbed Sweater with Mitred Neckline 1935

Just below waist-length boat-neck sweater with long or short set-in sleeves, in stocking stitch, with ribbed welts and neckline

★ Suitable for beginners

MATERIALS

Yarn
Sirdar Country Style DK
8(8:9) × 50g. balls

Needles
1 pair 3mm.
1 pair 3¾mm.

Buttons
2

MEASUREMENTS

Bust
87(92:97) cm.
34(36:38) in.

Length
56(57:58) cm.
22(22¼:22¾) in.

Sleeve Seam
45 cm.
17¾ in.

TENSION

12 sts. and 15 rows = 5cm. (2 in.) square over rib patt. when slightly stretched as in wear, using 3¾mm. needles. If your tension square does not correspond to these measurements, adjust the needle size used.

ABBREVIATIONS

k.=knit; p.=purl; st(s).=stitch(es); inc.= increase; dec.=decrease; beg.=begin(ning); rem. = remain(ing); rep. = repeat; alt. = alternate; tog. = together; sl. = slip stitch (transfer one stitch from left needle, knit-wise unless otherwise stated, to right hand needle.); cont. = continue; patt. = pattern; foll. = following; folls. = follows; mm. = millimetres; cm. = centimetre(s); in. = inch(es).

BACK

Cast on 119(127:135) sts. with 3mm. needles.
1st row: k.2, * p.1, k.1, rep. from * to last st., k.1.
2nd row: k.1, * p.1, k.1, rep. from * to end.
Rep. these 2 rows for 8 cm. (3¼ in.).
Change to 3¾mm. needles. Cont. in rib

until work measures 37 cm. (14½ in.), finishing after a wrong side row.

Shape Armholes
Cast off 4 sts. at beg. of next 2 rows, then dec. at both ends of every row until 95(99:103) sts. rem.
Cont. until work is 18(19:20) cm. (7(7½:7¾) in.) from beg. of armhole shaping, measured on the straight, finishing after a wrong side row.

Shape Shoulders
Cast off 9(10:11) sts. at beg. of next 4 rows and 9 sts. at beg. of foll. 2 rows. Cast off rem. 41 sts.

FRONT

Work as back to armholes.

Shape Armholes and Divide for Neck
Cast off 4 sts. at beg. of next 2 rows.
Next row: k.2 tog., work to end.
Next row: k.2 tog., work 50(54:58) sts. more, cast off central 7 sts., work to end.
Proceed on 1st set of 51(55:59) sts. for left side. Working neck edge straight, dec. 1st. at side edge every row until 44(46:48) sts. rem.
Cont. until work measures 12(13:14) cm. (4¾(5:5½)in.) from beg. of armhole.

Shape Neck
Dec. 1st. at neck edge on every row until 27(29:31) sts. rem.
Cont. until work matches back to outer shoulder.

Shape Shoulders
Cast off 9(10:11) sts. at beg. of next 2 side edge rows. Work to side edge. Cast off rem. 9 sts.
Join yarn to outer edge of rem. sts. and complete right side to correspond, reversing shapings.

SLEEVES

Cast on 55(59:63) sts. with 3mm. needles.
Work 8 cm. (3¼ in.) in k.1 p.1 rib. Change to 3¾mm. needles. Cont. in rib, inc. 1st. at both ends of next and every foll. 6th row until there are 87(91:95) sts. Cont. until work measures 45 cm. (17¾ in.), finishing after a wrong side row.

Shape Top
Cast off 4 sts. at beg. of next 2 rows. Dec. 1st. at both ends of next and every alt. row

until 47(51:55) sts. rem. Work 1 row. Dec. 1st. at both ends of every row until 39 sts. rem. Cast off 3 sts. at beg. of next 6 rows. Cast off rem. 21 sts.

NECKBAND

Cast on 157(165:173) sts. with 3mm. needles. Work 8 rows in k.1 p.1 rib.
Next row: make buttonholes thus – rib 11 sts., cast off 3 sts., rib 16 sts., cast off 3 sts., rib to end. In next row cast on 3 sts. over those cast off. Rib 8 rows. Cast off loosely in rib.

MAKING UP

Sew up side, shoulder and sleeve seams. Set sleeves into armholes. Mitre end of neckband at buttonhole end i.e. form a point by turning in corners of neckband end. See photographs.
Sew neckband to neck edge, lapping right over left at base. Press seams. Sew on buttons.

46

Wide-stripe Sweater

Hip-length, vertically-striped sweater with round neck, tight sleeves, ribbed welts and optional sewn-in shoulder pads

★★ Suitable for knitters with some previous experience

MATERIALS

Yarn
Patons Clansman 4 ply
3(4) × 50g. balls Col. A
4(5) × 50g. balls Col. B

Needles
1 pair 2¾mm.
1 pair 3¼mm.

Shoulder Pads (optional)
2

MEASUREMENTS

Bust
82/87(87/92) cm.
32/34(34/36) in.

Length
63(64) cm.
24¾(25) in.

Sleeve Seam
44(44) cm.
17¼(17¼) in.

TENSION

28 sts. and 36 rows = 10 cm. (4 in.) square over st. st. on 3¼mm. needles. If your tension square does not correspond to these measurements, adjust the needle size used.

ABBREVIATIONS

k.=knit; p.=purl; st(s).=stitch(es); inc.= increas(ing); dec.=decreas(ing); beg.= begin(ning); rem. = remain(ing); rep. = repeat; alt. = alternate; tog. = together; sl. = slip (transfer one stitch from left needle, knitwise unless otherwise stated, to right hand needle.); cont. = continue; patt. = pattern; foll. = following; folls. = follows; mm. = millimetres; cm. = centimetres; in. = inches; st. st. = stocking st.: one row k., one row p.; g. st. = garter st.: every row k.; incs. = increases; decs. = decreases.

BACK

Beg. at side edge.

Smaller size only:
** Cast on 63 sts. with A and 3¼mm. needles.
1st row: k.
2nd row: cast on 6 sts., p. to end.
Rep. 1st and 2nd rows twice more.
7th row: inc. in 1st st., k. to end.

8th row: as 2nd.
Now rep. 1st and 2nd rows twice more, and then 7th row once.
Break yarn and leave sts. on spare needle.
Now cast on 8 sts. with A and 3¼mm. needles.
1st row: p.
2nd row: cast on 6 sts., k. to end.
Rep. 1st and 2nd rows 3 more times.
Next row: p. to end, cast on 14 sts., now p. across sts. left on spare needle. [147 sts.]

Larger size only:
** Cast on 65 sts. with B and 3¼mm. needles.
1st row: k.
2nd row: cast on 6 sts., p. to end.
Rep. 1st and 2nd rows twice more.
Join in A.
7th row: with A, inc. in 1st st., k. to end.
8th row: with A, as 2nd.
Now rep. 1st and 2nd rows twice more, and then 7th row once.
Break yarn and leave sts. on spare needle.
Cast on 10 sts. with 3¼mm. needles and B.
1st row: p.
Join in A.
2nd row: with A, cast on 6 sts., k. to end.
3rd row: with A, p.
Rep. 2nd and 3rd rows twice more, and then 2nd row once.
Next row: p. to end, cast on 14 sts., now p. across sts. left on spare needle.
Work 4 rows.
Next row: inc. in 1st st., k. to end.
Work 1 row. [152 sts.]

Both sizes:
Cont. in stripes of 14 rows in B and 14 rows in A.
Work 4 rows.
Inc. 1 st. at beg. of next row, and then on every 6th row until there are 152(157) sts.
Work 5 rows, ending at neck edge. **

Shape Back Neck
Dec. 1 st. at neck edge on the next 4 rows.
Work 51 rows, ending with the 5th row of a B stripe.
Inc. 1 st. at neck edge on the next 4 rows.
*** Work 5 rows.
Dec. 1 st. at beg. of next row, and then every 6th row until 147(151) sts. rem.
Work 3 rows.
Next row: k.101(103) sts., cast off 14 sts., k. to end.
Cont. on last set of 32(34) sts.
1st row: p.
2nd row: cast off 6 sts., k. to end.
Rep. 1st and 2nd rows 3 times more.
Cast off rem. 8(10) sts.
Rejoin yarn to rem. sts.

1st row: cast off 6 sts., p. to end.
2nd row: k.2 tog., k. to end.
3rd row: as 1st.
4th row: k.
Rep. 3rd and 4th rows once more.
7th row: as 1st.
8th row: as 2nd.
Now rep. 3rd and 4th rows twice more.
Cast off rem. 63(65) sts.

FRONT

Work as for back from ** to **.

Shape Neck
Next row: cast off 6 sts., k. to end.
Now dec. 1 st. at neck edge on every row until 138(143) sts. rem., and then on every alt. row until 133(138) sts. rem.
Work 21 rows, thus ending with the 4th row of an A stripe.
Inc. 1 st. at neck edge on the next row, and then every alt. row until there are 139(144) sts.
Now inc. 1 st. at neck edge on every row until there are 146(151) sts.
Next row: cast on 6 sts., k. to end.
Now foll. back instructions from *** to end.

SLEEVES

Beg. at side edge.
Cast on 16 sts. with 3¼mm. needles and A.
1st row: k.
2nd row: cast on 8 sts., p. to last st., inc. 1.
Rep. 1st and 2nd rows 3(4) times more.
Cont. in st. st. and stripes of 14 rows in B and 14 rows in A.
Rep. 1st and 2nd rows 7(6) times more. [115(115) sts.]
Now keeping cuff edge straight, cont. to inc. for sleeve top on every alt. row until there are 118(119) sts. and then every 4th row until there are 122(123) sts.
Work 27 rows, thus ending with the 7th row of a B stripe.
Now dec. for sleeve top on next row, and then every 4th row until 117(118) sts. rem., and then every alt. row until 115(115) sts. rem.
Work 1 row.
Cont. as folls.:
1st row: cast off 8 sts., p. to last 2 sts., p.2 tog.
2nd row: k.
Rep. 1st and 2nd rows 9 times more, and then 1st row once.
Cast off rem. 16 sts.

BACK WELT

With right side of work facing, 2¾mm.

needles and B, k. up 129(139) sts. evenly along lower edge, i.e. 8 sts. for each 9 rows.

1st row: * k.1, p.1, rep. from * to last st., k.1.

2nd row: k.2, * p.1, k.1, rep. from * to last st., k.1.

Rep. 1st and 2nd rows for 8 cm. (3¼ in.). Cast off loosely in rib.

Work front welt to match.

CUFFS

With right side facing, 2¾mm. needles and B, k. up 57(61) sts. across sleeve edge, i.e. approx. 7 sts. for each 9 rows.

Work 8 cm. (3¼ in.) in rib as welts.

Cast off in rib.

MAKING UP

Press each piece lightly.

Sew up right shoulder seam.

Neck Border

With right side facing, 2¾mm. needles and B, k. up 25 sts. down left side of front neck edge, 17 sts. evenly from the 21 rows straight, 24 sts. up right side of neck, and 49 sts. evenly along back neck edge.

Work 9 rows in rib as for welts.

Cast off loosely in rib.

Sew up left shoulder and neck border seam.

Place a marker 18(19) cm. 7(7½ in.) to each side of shoulder seams to mark depth of armholes.

Sew up side and sleeve seams.

Sew sleeves to armhole edges.

Press seams.

Sew shoulder pads into position.

Fold cuffs onto right side.

Long, Lean Angora Sweater

Long, fine sweater in stocking stitch with raised rib yoke, set-in sleeves and pocket

★★ Suitable for knitters with some previous experience

MATERIALS

Yarn
Pingouin Oued
6(6:6:7) × 50g. balls

Needles
1 pair 2¾mm.
1 pair 3¾mm.

MEASUREMENTS

Bust
87(92:97:102) cm.
34(36:38:40) in.

Length
60(61:62:63) cm.
23¾(24:24¼:24¾) in.

Sleeve Seam
43(44:45:46) cm.
16¾(17¼:17¾:18) in.

TENSION

27 sts. and 32 rows = 10 cm. (4 in.) square

over st. st. using 3¾mm. needles. If your tension square does not correspond to these measurements, adjust the needle size used.

ABBREVIATIONS

k.=knit; p.=purl; st(s).=stitch(es); inc.= increas(ing); dec.=decreas(ing); beg.= begin(ning); rem. = remain(ing); rep. = repeat; alt. = alternate; tog. = together; sl. = slip (transfer one stitch from left needle, knitwise unless otherwise stated, to right hand needle.); cont. = continue; patt. = pattern; foll. = following; folls. = follows; mm. = millimetres; cm. = centimetres; in. = inches; st. st. = stocking st.: one row k., one row p.; g. st. = garter st.: every row k.; incs. = increases; decs. = decreases.

BACK

Cast on 120(128:136:144) sts. with 2¾mm. needles.

Work 5 cm. (2 in.) in k.1, p.1 rib.

Change to 3¾mm. needles and st. st.

Cont. until work measures 41(42:42:43)

cm. (16(16½:16½:16¾) in.), ending with a p. row.

Shape Armholes
Cast off 5(6:7:8) sts. at beg. of next 2 rows.

Dec. 1 st. at each end of next 4 rows.

Dec. 1 st. at each end of next and every foll. alt. row until 92(96:100:104) sts. rem. Work 1 row.
Change to rib patt. as folls.:
1st row (right side): k.
2nd row: k.3(2:1:0), * p.2, k.4, rep. from * to last 5(4:3:2) sts., p.2, k.3(2:1:0).
These 2 rows form rib patt.
Cont. in patt. until work measures 60(61:62:63) cm. (23¾(24:24¼:24¾) in.)

Shape Shoulders
Cast off 6 sts. at beg. of next 2 rows.
Cast off 6(6:7:7) sts. at beg. of next 2 rows.
Cast off 6(7:7:7) sts. at beg. of next 2 rows.
Cast off 7(7:7:8) sts. at beg. of next 2 rows.
Cast off rem. 42(44:46:48) sts.

FRONT

Work as for back until work measures 36 cm. (14 in.), ending with a p. row.
Cont. as folls.:
1st row: k.
2nd row: p.58(62:66:70), k.1, p.2, k.1, p.58(62:66:70).
3rd and alt. rows: k.
4th row: p.57(61:65:69), k.2, p.2, k.2, p.57(61:65:69).
6th row: p.56(60:64:68), k.3, p.2, k.3, p.56(60:64:68).
8th row: p.55(59:63:67), k.4, p.2, k.4, p.55(59:63:67).
10th and 12th rows: as 8th.
14th row: p.52(56:60:64), k.1, p.2, k.4, p.2, k.4, p.2, k.1, p.52(56:60:64).
Cont. inc. rib patt. by one st. on each side, on alt. rows until work measures same as back to armhole.

Shape Armholes
Work as for back, keeping rib patt. enlarging correct.
Cont. until armhole shapings are completed. [92(96:100:104) sts.]
Change to rib patt. across all sts.
Cont. in rib patt. until work measures 53(54:54:55) cm. (20¾(21¼:21¼:21½) in.).

Shape Neck
1st row: patt. 36(38:39:41), cast off 20(20:22:22) sts., patt. to end.
Now work on 2nd set of 36(38:39:41) sts.
Dec. 1 st. at neck edge on next 6 rows.
Now dec. 1 st. at neck edge on alt. rows until 25(26:27:28) sts. rem.
Cont. without shaping until work measures same as back to shoulder, ending at armhole edge.

Shape Shoulder
Cast off 6 sts. at beg. of next row.
Work 1 row.
Cast off 6(6:7:7) sts. at beg. of next row.
Work 1 row.
Cast off 6(7:7:7) sts. at beg. of next row.
Work 1 row.
Cast off rem. 7(7:7:8) sts.
Rejoin yarn to neck edge of rem. 36(38:39:41) sts. and work to match first side.

SLEEVES

Cast on 52(52:58:58) sts. with 2¾mm.

needles.
Work 7 cm. (2¾ in.) in k.1, p.1 rib.
Change to 3¾mm. needles and rib patt.:
1st row: k.
2nd row: * k.4, p.2, rep. from * to last 4 sts., k.4.
Cont. in patt., inc. 1 st. at each end of 5th and every foll. 6th row until there are 94(94:100:100) sts., working inc. sts. into patt.
Cont. without shaping until work measures 43(44:45:46) cm. (16¾(17¼: 17¾:18) in.).

Shape Top
Cast off 5(3:3:3) sts. at beg. of next 2(4:4:4) rows.
Dec. 1 st. at each end of next 4 rows.

Dec. 1 st. at each end of next and every foll. alt. row until 46(44:48:46) sts. rem.
Dec. 1 st. at each end of next 4 rows.
Cast off 4 sts. at beg. of next 6 rows.
Cast off.

POCKET
Cast on 46 sts. with 3¾mm. needles.
Work in rib patt. as folls.:
1st row: k.
2nd row: * k.4, p.2, rep. from * to last 4 sts., k.4.
Cont. until work measures 15 cm. (5¾ in.).
Cast off.

NECKBAND
Sew up right shoulder seam.

With 2¾mm. needles, pick up and k.30(32:34:36) sts. from side front neck, 20(20:22:22) sts. from centre front neck, 30(32:34:36) sts. from side front neck and 44(44:46:46) sts. from back neck. [124(128:136:140) sts.].
Work 5 cm. (2 in.) in k.1, p.1 rib.
Cast off loosely in rib.

MAKING UP
Sew up left shoulder and neckband seam.
Sew up side and sleeve seams.
Set in sleeves.
Fold neckband in half to inside and slip st. into place.
Place pocket at desired position and slip st. into place.

Leafy, Openwork Cardigan

Lightweight cardigan in openwork design, with set-in sleeves, ribbed round neck, hem and cuffs, moss-stitch front bands

★★ Suitable for knitters with some previous experience

MATERIALS
Yarn
Pingouin Pingolaine
6(7:7:8) × 50g. balls

Needles
1 pair 2¾mm.
1 pair 3¼mm.

Buttons
7

MEASUREMENTS
Bust
79–84(87–92:94–99:102–107) cm.
31–33(34–36:37–39:40–42) in.

Length
56(56:57:57) cm.
22(22:22¼:22¼) in.

Sleeve Seam
45 cm.
17¾ in.

TENSION
26 sts. and 38 rows = 10 cm. (4 in.) square over patt. with 3¼mm. needles. If your tension square does not correspond to these measurements, adjust the needle size used.

ABBREVIATIONS
k.=knit; p.=purl; st(s).=stitch(es); inc.= increase; dec.=decrease; beg.=begin(ning); rem. = remain(ing); rep. = repeat; alt. = alternate; tog. = together; sl. = slip stitch (transfer one stitch from left needle, knit-wise unless otherwise stated, to right hand needle.); cont. = continue; patt. = pattern; foll. = following; folls. = follows; mm. = millimetres; cm. = centimetres; in. = inch(es); st.st. = stocking stitch; m.st. = moss stitch; y.fwd. = yarn forward; tog. = together; t.b.l. through back of loops.

BACK
Cast on 105(115:125:135) sts. with 2¾mm. needles and work in k.1, p.1 rib, beg. and ending right side rows with p.1, and wrong side rows with k.1.
Cont. until work measures 5 cm. (2 in.) from beg., ending with a right side row. Change to 3¼mm. needles and p.1 row on wrong side, working 7 incs. evenly, spaced across it.
Cont. on these 112(122:132:142) sts. in patt.

1st row: k.2, * y.fwd., k.2, k.2 tog., k.2 tog., t.b.l., k.2, y.fwd., k.2, rep. from * to end.
2nd and alt. rows: p.
3rd row: k.3, * y.fwd., k.1, k.2 tog. k.2 tog. t.b.l., k.1, y.fwd., k.4, rep. from * ending last rep. k.3.
5th row: k.4, * y.fwd., k.2 tog., k.2 tog. t.b.l., y.fwd., k.6, rep. from * ending last rep. k.4.
7th row: k.1, * k.2 tog. t.b.l., k.2, (y.fwd., k.2) twice, k.2 tog., rep. from * to last st., k.1.

9th row: k.1, * k.2 tog. t.b.l., k.1, y.fwd., k.4, y.fwd., k.1, k.2 tog., rep. from * to last st., k.1.
11th row: k.1, * k.2 tog. t.b.l., y.fwd., k.6, y.fwd., k.2 tog., rep. from * to last st., k.1.
12th row: p.
These 12 rows form one patt.
Cont. in patt. until work measures 37 cm. (14½ in.) from beg., ending with a p. row.

Shape Armholes
Cast off 3 sts. at beg. of next 2 rows, 2 sts. at beg. of next 4 rows and 1 st. at beg. of next 6 rows. [92(102:112:122) sts.]
Cont. without shaping until work measures 56(56:57:57) cm. (22(22: 22¼:22¼) in.) from beg., ending with a p. row.

Shape Shoulder
Cast off 8(10:10:12) sts. at beg. of next 4 rows and 11(11:15:15) sts. at beg. of next 2 rows.
Cast off rem. 38(40:42:44) sts. for back neck.

RIGHT FRONT

Cast on 53(59:63:69) sts. with 2¾mm. needles and work in rib with m.st. border:

1st row (right side): k.1, * p.1, k.1, rep. from * to end.
2nd row: * p.1, k.1, rep. from * to last 11 sts., (k.1, p.1) 5 times, k.1.
Cont. in this way until you have worked 8(8:10:10) rows then make buttonhole.
Next row: m.st. 4, cast off 3, work to end.
Next row: cast on 3 sts. over buttonhole.
Make 5 more buttonholes at intervals of 9 cm. (3½ in.), throughout work. At same time cont. until work measures 5 cm. (2 in.) from beg., ending with a first row.
Change to 3¼mm. needles.
Next row: p.42(48:52:58) sts., working 5(4:5:4) incs. evenly spaced during this section, then m.st. rem. 11 sts.
Cont. on these 58(63:68:73) sts., working in patt. with m.st. border.

First and Third sizes:
1st row: m.st.11, k.1, k.2 tog. t.b.l., k.2, y.fwd., k.2, then rep. from * in 1st patt. row above, to end.
2nd and alt. rows: p. to last 11 sts., m.st.11.
Second and Fourth sizes:
1st row: m.st.11, k.2, then rep. from * in 1st patt. row (after right front) to end.
2nd and alt. rows: p. to last 11 sts., m.st.11.
All sizes:
Cont. in patt. as now set noting that for first and third sizes you have a half-patt. at front edge after the m.st. border.

Cont. until you have worked 1 more row than on back to armhole, thus ending at side edge.

Shape Armhole
Cast off 3 sts. at beg. of next row, 2 sts. at same edge on next 2 alt. rows and 1 st. on next 3 alt. rows.
Cont. on rem. 48(53:58:63) sts. until work measures 52(52:53:53) cm. (20½(20½: 20¾:20¾) in.) from beg., ending at front edge.

Shape Neck and Shouler
Next row: m.st.11 and place these sts. on a safety pin, cast off 3(3:4:4) sts., patt. to end.
Cont. in patt. and cast off at neck edge on alt. rows 2 sts. 2(3:3:4) times and 1 st. 3(2:2:1) times.
Cont. on rem. 27(31:35:39) sts. until work matches back to shoulder, ending at armhole edge.
Cast off 8(10:10:12) sts. at beg. of next row and next alt. row.
Work 1 row, then cast off rem. 11(11:15:15) sts.

LEFT FRONT
Cast on 53(59:63:69) sts. with 2¾mm. needles and work in rib with m.st. border.
1st row: * k.1, p.1, rep. from * to last st., k.1.

2nd row: k.1, (p.1, k.1) 5 times, * k.1, p.1, rep. from * to end.
Rep. these 2 rows until work measures 5 cm. (2 in.), ending with a first row.
Change to 3¼mm. needles.
Next row: m.st.11, then p. to end, working 5(4:5:4) incs. evenly spaced.
Cont. on these 58(63:68:73) sts. in patt. with m.st. border.
1st row: k.2, then rep. from * in first patt. row 4(5:5:6) times in all, then for first and third sizes only, y.fwd., k.2, k.2 tog., k.1, then for all sizes m.st.11.
Cont. in patt. as now set keeping m.st. border at front edge and noting that for first and third sizes you have an extra half-patt. at front edge inside this border. Complete as for right front, reversing all shapings, and omitting buttonholes.

SLEEVES

Cast on 63(63:71:71) sts. with 2¾mm. needles and work in k.1, p.1, rib for 5 cm. (2 in.), ending with a right side row.
Change to 3¼mm. needles and p.1 row working 19(19:21:21) incs. evenly spaced across it. [82(82:92:92) sts.]
Now work in patt. as for back but inc. 1 st. at both ends of every foll. 16th(16th:20th:20th) row 8(8:6:6) times, working extra sts. into patt. where possible, or keeping them in st.st. if they cannot be worked into patt.
Cont. on 98(98:104:104) sts. until work measures 45 cm. (17¾ in.) from beg.

Shape Top
Cast off 3 sts. at beg. of next 2 rows, 2 sts. at beg. of next 4 rows, 1 st. at beg. of next 20(20:22:22) rows and 2 sts. at beg. of next 20(20:22:22) rows. Cast off rem. 24 sts.

NECKBAND
Sew up shoulder seams.
Place sts. of right front border onto a 2¾mm. needle so that point is at inner edge, rejoin yarn, and with right side facing pick up and k.81(83:87:89) sts. evenly round neck edge, then work in m.st. on the 11 sts. of left front border.
Next row: m.st.11, * k.1, p.1, rep. from * to last 12 sts., k.1, m.st.11.
Cont. thus in rib with m.st. borders, work 4 more rows then make buttonhole at right front edge on next 2 rows.
Work 5 more rows. Cast off.

MAKING UP

Sew in sleeves matching centre of sleeve head to shoulder seam.
Sew up side and sleeve seams.
Sew on buttons. Press as instructions on ball band.

Classic Round-neck Cardigan

 1980

Loose-fitting, simple cardigan with knitted-in pockets, set-in sleeves, ribbed front bands and welts, in stocking stitch

★ Suitable for beginners

MATERIALS

Yarn
Emmerdale DK
9(10:11:12) × 50g. balls
or
Poppleton Emmerdale Chunky
11(12:13:14) × 40g. balls

Needles
1 pair 4½mm.
1 pair 6mm.
1 stitch holder

Buttons
7

MEASUREMENTS

Bust
82(87:92:97) cm.
32(34:36:38) in.

Length
52(53:54:55) cm.
20½(20¾:21¼:21½) in.

Sleeve Seam
43(43:44:44) cm.
16¾(16¾:17¼:17¼) in.

TENSION

7½ sts. and 9½ rows = 5 cm. (2 in.) square over stocking stitch on 6mm. needles. If your tension square does not correspond to these measurements, adjust the needle size used.

ABBREVIATIONS

k.=knit; p.=purl; st(s).=stitch(es); inc.= increase; dec.=decrease; beg.=begin(ning); rem. = remain(ing); rep. = repeat; alt. = alternate; tog. = together; sl. = slip stitch (transfer one stitch from left needle, knit-wise unless otherwise stated, to right hand needle.); cont. = continue; patt. = pattern; foll. = following; folls. = follows; mm. = millimetres; cm. = centimetre(s); in. = inch(es); st.st., = stocking stitch; m.1 = increase 1 st. by picking up loop from between needles and knitting into the back of it; y.r.n. = yarn round needle.

LEFT FRONT

** Pocket Lining
Cast on 17 sts. with 6mm. needles.
Work 17 rows in st.st., starting with a p. row.
Break yarn and leave sts. on spare needle

or stitch holder.
Now cast on 31(33:35:37) sts. with 4½mm. needles.
1st row: k.2, *p.1, k.1, rep. from * to last st., k.1.
2nd row: *k.1, p.1, rep. from * to last st., k.1.
Rep. 1st and 2nd rows 4 times more.
Change to 6mm. needles and st.st., starting with a k. row.
Work 18 rows.

Make Pocket
Next row: k.7(8:9:10) sts., slip next 17 sts. on to a stitch holder and k. pocket lining sts. in place of these, k. to end.
Cont. until front measures 35(35:36:36) cm. (13¾(13¾:14:14) in.) from beg. ending at side edge.**

Shape Armhole
Next row: cast off 3(3:4:4) sts. k. to end.

Work 1 row.
Now dec. 1 st. at beg. of next row, and then every alt. row until 25(26:27:28) sts. rem.
Work 9(9:9:9) rows, ending with a p. row.

Shape Neck
Next row: k. to last 4 sts., cast off these sts. Break yarn.
Turn and rejoin yarn at neck edge.
Dec. 1 st. at neck edge on the next 4 rows, and the 4 foll. alt. rows.
Work 3 rows, ending at armhole edge.

Shape Shoulder
Cast off 4(5:5:5) sts. at beg. of next row,

and 5(4:5:6) sts. at beg. of foll. alt. row.
Work 1 row.
Cast off 4(5:5:5) rem. sts.

Pocket Border
Slip sts. from stitch holder on to a 4½mm. needle.
1st row: k.1, * m.1, (p.1, k.1) twice, p.1, rep. from * twice more, m.1, k.1. [21 sts.]
2nd row: * k.1, p.1, rep. from * to last st., k.1.
3rd row: k.2, * p.1, k.1, rep. from * to last st., k.1.
Rep. 2nd and 3rd rows once more.
Cast off in rib.

RIGHT FRONT

Follow instructions for left from ** to **, working 1 row more to end at side edge.

Shape Armhole
Next row: cast off 3(3:4:4) sts., p. to end.
Now dec. 1 st. at end of next row, and then every alt. row until 25(26:27:28) sts. rem.
Work 9(9:9:9) rows, ending with a p. row.

Shape Neck
Next row: cast off 4 sts., k. to end.
Now complete to match left front, beg. with row starting 'Dec. 1 st.', working 1 extra row before shaping shoulder.
Work pocket border as left front.

BACK

Cast on 65(69:73:77) sts. with 4½mm. needles and work 10 rows in rib as left front.
Change to 6mm. needles and st.st.
Work until back measures same as fronts to armholes, ending with a p. row.

Shape Armholes
Cast off 3(3:4:4) sts. at beg. of next 2 rows.
Now dec. 1 st. at each end of next row, and then every alt. row until 53(55:57:59) sts. rem.
Work until armholes measure same as fronts, ending with a p. row.

Shape Shoulders and Back of Neck
Next row: cast off 4(5:5:5) sts., k.12(12:13:14) sts. including st. on needle, cast off 21 sts., k. to end.
Cont. on last set of sts.
1st row: cast off 4(5:5:5) sts., p. to last 2 sts., p.2 tog.
2nd row: k.2 tog., k. to end.
3rd row: cast off 5(4:5:6) sts., p. to last 2 sts., p.2 tog.

4th row: k.
Cast off 4(5:5:5) rem. sts.
Rejoin yarn to rem. sts. at neck edge.
1st row: p.2 tog. p. to end.
2nd row: cast off 5(4:5:6) sts., k. to last 2
sts., k.2 tog.
3rd row: as 1st row.
Cast off 4(5:5:5) rem. sts.

SLEEVES

Cast on 33(33:35:35) sts. with 4½mm.
needles and work 10 rows in rib as left
front.
Change to 6mm. needles and st.st.
Work 4 rows.
Inc. 1 st. at each end of next row, and then
every 12th (10th:10th:8th) row until there
are 45(47:49:51) sts.
Work until sleeve measures 43(43:44:44)
cm. (16¾(16¾:17¼:17¼) in.) from beg.,
ending with a p. row.

Shape Top

Cast off 3(3:4:4) sts. at beg. of next 2 rows.
Now dec. 1 st. at each end of next row,
and then every alt. row until 21(21:21:21)
sts. rem., and then every row until 13 sts.
rem.
Cast off.

NECK AND FRONT BANDS

Press each piece lightly with cool iron and
dry cloth.
Join shoulder seams.

Neckband

With 4½mm. needles, and with right side
of work facing, k. up 22 sts. along right
front neck edge, 23 sts. evenly along back
neck edge, and 22 sts. along left front neck
edge.
1st row: * k.1, p.1, rep. from * to last st.,
k.1.
2nd row: k.2, * p.1, k.1, rep. from * to the
last st., k.1.
Rep. 1st and 2nd rows once more, and
then 1st row once.
Cast off in rib.

Left Front Band

Cast on 8 sts. with 4½mm. needles.
1st row: (k.1, p.1) 3 times, k.2.
2nd row: (k.1, p.1) 4 times.
These 2 rows form rib.
Work until band is long enough to fit up
left front edge when slightly stretched,
ending with 2nd row.
Cast off firmly in rib.
Sew band to front.

Pin the positions of 7 buttons on band, the
bottom button in 5th row from cast on
edge, the top button in 3rd row from cast
off edge, and the rest equally spaced between.

Right front band

Cast on 8 sts. with 4½mm. needles.
1st row: k.2, (p.1, k.1) 3 times.
2nd row: (p.1, k.1) 4 times.
These 2 rows form rib.
Work 2 more rows.
Make buttonhole: k.2, p.1, y.r.n., p.2 tog.,
k.1, p.1, k.1.
Making buttonholes in this way to correspond with marked positions, work until
border measures same as left side, ending
with 2nd row.
Cast off firmly in rib.

MAKING UP

Sew right front band to front.
Sew up side and sleeve seams.
Sew sleeves into armholes.
Sew pocket linings and pocket borders in
position.
Press seams lightly.
Sew on buttons.

Diagonal Pattern Shirt Blouse

Fine wool, yoked shirt blouse with buttoned front placket and collar,
reaching just below the waist, worked in diagonal rib pattern

★★ Suitable for knitters with some
previous experience

MATERIALS

Yarn
Wendy Shetland 4 ply
11(11:12) × 25g. balls

Needles
1 pair 2¾mm. 1 pair 3¼mm.
1 set of 4 3¼mm. (pointed each end)

Buttons
2

MEASUREMENTS

Bust
87(92:97) cm.
34(36:38) in.

Length
49(52:54) cm.
19¼(20½:21¼) in.

Sleeve Seam
49.5 cm.
19½ in.

TENSION

27 sts. and 36 rows = 10 cm. (4 in.) square
over diagonal rib on 3¼mm. needles. If
your tension square does not correspond

ABBREVIATIONS

k.=knit; p.=purl; st(s).=stitch(es); inc.=
increase; dec.=decrease; beg.=begin(ning);
rem.=remain(ing); rep.=repeat; alt.=
alternate; tog.=together; sl.=slip stitch
(transfer one stitch from left needle, knit-
wise unless otherwise stated, to right

hand needle.); cont. = continue; patt. = pattern; foll. = following; folls. = follows; mm. = millimetres; cm. = centimetre(s); in. = inch(es); g.st = garter stitch.

BACK

Cast on 128(136:144) sts. using 2¾mm. needles.
Work in k.3, p.1 rib as folls. for 5 cm. (2 in.).
1st row: * k.3, p.1, rep. from * to end.
2nd row: * k.1, p.3, rep. from * to end.
Change to 3¼mm. needles and diagonal rib as folls.:
1st row: * k.3, p.1, rep. from * to end.
2nd row: * k.1, p.3, rep. from * to end.
3rd row: * k.2, p.1, k.1, rep. from * to end.
4th row: * p.1, k.1, p.2, rep. from * to end.
5th row: * k.1, p.1, k.2, rep. from * to end.
6th row: * p.2, k.1, p.1, rep. from * to end.
7th row: * p.1, k.3, rep. from * to end.
8th row: * p.3, k.1, rep. from * to end.
These 8 rows form the patt.
Cont. straight until work measures 27 cm. (10½ in.), ending with a wrong side row.

Shape Armholes

Cast off 9 sts. at beg. of next 2 rows, then dec. 1 st. at beg. of foll. 8 rows [102(110:118) sts.]
Leave sts. on a spare needle.

measures 27 cm. (10½ in.), ending with a wrong side row.

Shape Armhole

Cast off 9 sts. at beg. of next row, then dec. 1 st. at beg. of foll. 4 alt. rows, [53(57:61) sts.]
Patt. 1 row and leave sts. on a spare needle.
Cast on 2 sts., patt. across sts. left on spare needle, beg. at centre front, to end.
Complete to match left side reversing shaping and omitting last row.

SLEEVES

Cast on 47(47:51) sts. using 2¾mm. needles and work 11 cm.(4¼ in.) in k.3, p.1 rib, arranging sts. as folls.:
1st row: * k.3, p.1, rep. from * to last 3 sts. k.3.
2nd row: * p.3, k.1, rep. from * to last 3 sts., p.3.
Change to 3¼mm. needles and diagonal rib, inc. 1 st. each end of every 6th row until there are 87(87:95) sts.
Cont. straight until work measures 49.5 cm. (19½ in.), ending with a wrong side row.

Shape Top

Cast off 19 sts. at beg. of next 2 rows.
Leave rem. 49(49:57) sts. on spare needle.
Work second sleeve in same way.

YOKE

With four 3¼mm. needles and right side facing, rejoin yarn to right side of front, k.2, work in k.3, p.1 rib across the sts. of right front, sleeve, back, left sleeve and left front to last 2 sts., k.2. [306(322:354) sts.]
Next row: k.2, k.2 tog., rib 71(75:83) sts., p.2 tog., k.1, p.2 tog., rib 146(154:170) sts., p.2 tog., k.1, p.2 tog., rib to last 4 sts., k.2 tog., k.2.

Next row: k.2, rib to last 2 sts., k.2.
Next row: k.2, k.2 tog., rib (69:73:81) sts., p.2 tog., k.1, p.2 tog., rib 144(152:168) sts., p.2 tog., k.1, p.2 tog., rib to last 4 sts., k.2 tog., k.2.
Next row: k.2, rib to last 2 sts., k.2.
Keeping rib correct, cont. to dec. 6 sts. on alt. rows in this way until 222(232:258) sts. rem., ending with a wrong side row.

Shape Shoulders and Neck

Work 51(53:59) sts., turn.
Leave rem. 171(179:199) sts. on spare needle.
Complete right front as folls.:
1st row: cast off 2 sts., rib to last 4 sts., k.2 tog., k.2.
2nd row: patt. to end.
Rep. these 2 rows until 12(14:20) sts. rem.
Cont. casting off 2 sts. at shoulder edge on every alt. row until 2 sts. rem. Cast off.
With right side facing, rejoin yarn to sts. left on spare needle. Cast off 2 sts., rib 117(123:137) sts., turn.
Leave rem. 51(53:59) sts. on a spare needle.
Complete back as folls.:
Cast off 2 sts. at beg. of every row until 44(44:48) sts. rem.
Next row: * k.2, k.2 tog., rep. from * to end.
Cast off.
With right side facing, rejoin yarn to sts. left on spare needle.
Cast off 2 sts., rib to last 2 sts., k.2.
Complete to match right front, reversing shapings.

COLLAR

Cast on 14 sts. using 2¾mm. needles.
Working in g.st. throughout, cont. straight until work measures 3 cm. (1¼ in.).
Work buttonhole: k.6, cast off 2 sts., k. to end.
Next row: cast on 2 sts. over those cast off in previous row.
When work measures 7 cm. (2¾ in.), work second buttonhole, repeating two buttonhole rows above.
Next row: k.6, inc. in next st., k. to end.
Inc. 1 st. in the centre of work every 6(7:7.5) cm. (2¼(2¾:3) in.) until 18 sts. are obtained. Work 23(24:24) cm. (9(9½:9½) in.) straight, then dec. 1 st. in the centre of work on next row and every foll. 6(7:7.5) cm. (2¼(2¾:3) in.), until 14 sts. rem. Cast off.

MAKING UP

Sew up shoulder seams. Sew up sleeve under-arm.
Sew up sleeve and side seams.
Attach collar (left side of collar will end at neck slit), with neat slipstitch on right side, so that seam will be hidden by collar.
Sew on buttons.

FRONT

Work as given for back until work measures 23 cm. (9 in.), ending with a wrong side row.
Divide for front opening:
Patt. 64(68:72) sts., turn. Leave rem. sts. on a spare needle.
Complete left side as folls.:
Cast on 2 sts., k.2, patt. to end.
Cont. straight, working the 2 cast on sts. in g.st. and rest in patt., until work

Wartime Forces' Polo-neck Sweater 1942

Simplest, unisex, stocking-stitch, polo-neck sweater with set-in sleeves and ribbed welts, designed as forces' wartime comfort

★ Suitable for beginners

MATERIALS

Yarn
Patons Clansman 4 ply
8(8:9:9:9) × 50g. balls

Needles
1 pair 2¾mm.
1 pair 3¼mm.
1 set of 4 double-pointed 2¾mm.

MEASUREMENTS

Chest
92(97:102:107:112) cm.
36(38:40:42:44) in.

Length
63(65:66:67:69) cm.
24¾(25½:26:26¼:27) in.

Sleeve Seam
46(46:47:47:48) cm.
18(18:18½:18½:18¾) in.

TENSION

28 sts. and 36 rows = 10 cm. (4 in.) square over st.st. on 3¼mm. needles. If your tension square does not correspond to these measurements, adjust the needle size used.

ABBREVIATIONS

k.=knit; p.=purl; st(s).=stitch(es); inc.= increase; dec.=decrease; beg.=begin(ning); rem. = remain(ing); rep. = repeat; alt. = alternate; tog. = together; sl. = slip stitch (transfer one stitch from left needle, knitwise unless otherwise stated, to right hand needle.); cont. = continue; patt. = pattern; foll. = following; folls. = follows; mm. = millimetres; cm. = centimetres; in. = inch(es); st.st. = stocking stitch.

BACK

Cast on 127(135:141:149:155) sts. with 2¾mm. needles.
1st row: k.2, * p.1, k.1, rep. from * to last st., k.1.
2nd row: k.1, * p.1, k.1, rep. from * to end.
These 2 rows form rib.
Cont. until work measures 10 cm. (4 in.), ending after 2nd row and inc. 6 sts. during last row. [133(141:147:155:161) sts.]

Change to 3¼mm. needles and st.st., beg. with a k. row.
Cont. until work measures 42 cm. (16½ in.), ending after a p. row.

Shape Armholes

Cast off 8(9:10:11:12) sts. at beg. of next 2 rows.
Dec. 1 st. at each end of next 7(7:7:9:9) rows, then at each end of every alt. row until 95(99:103:107:111) sts. rem. **
Cont. straight until back measures 63(65:66:67:69) cm. (24¾(25½:26:26¼: 27) in.) at centre, ending after a p. row.

Shape Shoulders

Cast off 9(10:10:10:11) sts. at beg. of next 4 rows, then 10(9:10:11:10) sts. at beg. of next 2 rows.
Leave rem. 39(41:43:45:47) sts. on a spare needle.

FRONT

Work as back to **.
Work straight until front measures 54(56: 57:57:58) cm. (21¼(22:22¼:22¼:22¾) in.) at centre, ending after a p. row.

Shape Neck

Next row: k.33(34:35:36:37), turn. Cont. on this group.
Dec. 1 st. at neck edge on next 5 rows. [28(29:30:31:32) sts.]
Work straight until front measures same

as back to shoulder, ending at armhole edge.

Shape Shoulder

Cast off 9(10:10:10:11) sts. at beg. of next row and foll. alt. row.
Work 1 row. Cast off.
With right side facing, slip centre 29(31: 33:35:37) sts. onto a spare needle.
Rejoin yarn to sts. left for other side and complete to match first half.

SLEEVES

Cast on 59(61:63:65:67) sts. with 2¾mm. needles and work 10 cm. (4 in.) in k.1, p.1 rib as for back, ending after a 1st row.
Next row: rib 5(3:4:2:3), * inc. in next st., rib 11(8:8:5:4), rep. from * to last 6(4:5:3:4) sts., inc. in next st., rib to end. [64(68:70: 76:80) sts.]
Change to 3¼mm. needles and st.st.
Inc. 1 st. at each end of 9th row, then at each end of every foll. 6th row until there are 84(88:94:100:108) sts., then at each end of every foll. 8th row until there are 96(100: 106:110:116) sts.
Cont. straight until work measures 46(46: 47:47:48) cm., (18(18:18½:18½:18¾) in.), ending after a p. row.

Shape Sleeve Top

Cast off 8(9:10:11:12) sts. at beg. of next 2 rows.
Work 2(4:4:6:6) rows straight.
Dec. 1 st. at each end of every k. row until 42 sts. rem.
Dec. 1 st. at each end of every row until 28 sts. rem.
Cast off.

POLO COLLAR

Sew up shoulder seams.
With set of 2¾mm. needles, k. across back sts., pick up and knit 29(29:29:33:33) sts. down left side of front, knit across the sts. on spare needle, pick up and knit 29(29: 29:33:33) sts. up right side of front. [126(130:134:146:150) sts.]
Work 19 cm. (7½ in.) in k.1, p.1 rib.
Cast off loosely in rib.

MAKING UP

Omitting ribbing, press, following instructions on the ball band.
Sew up side and sleeve seams.
Set in sleeves. Press seams.

Cashmere, Square-neck Twin Set 1980

Squared twin set with set-in sleeves, ribbed hem welts, cardigan with left front pocket and mitred, stocking stitch borders

★★ Suitable for knitters with some previous experience

MATERIALS

Yarn
Yarn Store Cashmere
Cardigan:
13(14:15:16:17) × 20g. hanks
Sweater:
13(14:15:16:17) × 20g. hanks

Needles
1 pair 2¾mm.
1 pair 3¼mm.
st. holder

MEASUREMENTS

Bust (both)
82(87:92:97:102) cm.
32(34:36:38:40) in.

Length (cardigan)
62 cm.
24¼ in.

Length (sweater)
60 cm.
23¾ in.

Sleeve Seam (both)
44 cm.
17¼ in.

TENSION

28 sts. and 36 rows = 10 cm. (4 in.) square over st. st. on 3¼mm. needles. If your tension square does not correspond to these measurements, adjust the needle size used.

ABBREVIATIONS

k.=knit; p.=purl; st(s).=stitch(es); inc.= increas(ing); dec.=decreas(ing); beg.= begin(ning); rem. = remain(ing); rep. = repeat; alt. = alternate; tog. = together; sl. = slip (transfer one stitch from left needle, knitwise unless otherwise stated, to right hand needle.); cont. = continue; patt. = pattern; foll. = following; folls. = follows; mm. = millimetres; cm. = centimetres; in. = inches; st. st. = stocking st.: one row k., one row p.; g. st. = garter st.: every row k.; incs. = increases; decs. = decreases.

CARDIGAN BACK

Cast on 114(122:128:136:142) sts. with 2¾mm. needles.
Work 23 rows in k.2, p.2 rib.
Inc. row: rib 8(12:8:12:11) sts., * inc. in next st., rib 13(13:15:15:16), rep. from * to last 8(12:8:12:12) sts., inc. in next st., rib 7(11:7:11:11). [122(130:136:144:150) sts.]
Change to 3¼mm. needles.
Cont. in st. st. (k. the first row) until work measures 44(43:43:42:41) cm. (17¼(16¾: 16¾:16½:16) in.). ending with a p. row.

Shape Armholes
Cast off 5 sts. at beg. of next 2 rows.
Dec. 1 st. at each end of next 5 rows, then every foll. alt. row 4(5:5:6:6) times. [94(100:106:112:118) sts.]
Cont. straight until armholes measure 18(19:19:20:21) cm. (7(7½:7½:7¾:8¼) in.), ending with a p. row.

Shape Shoulders
Cast off 5(5:5:6:6) sts. at beg. of next 6 rows and 4(6:8:7:9) sts. on foll. 2 rows.
Sl. rem. 56(58:60:62:64) sts. onto a spare needle.

CARDIGAN POCKET LINING

Cast on 24 sts. with 3¼mm. needles.
Work 22 rows in st. st.
Sl. sts. onto a spare needle.

CARDIGAN LEFT FRONT

Cast on 52(56:60:64:66) sts. with 2¾mm. needles.
Work 23 rows in k.2, p.2 rib.
Inc. row: rib 6(7:8:8:9), * inc. in next st., rib 12(13:14:15:15), rep. from * to last 7(7:7:8:9) sts., inc. in next st., rib 6(6:6: 7:8). [56(60:64:68:70) sts.]
Change to 3¼mm. needles.
Cont. in st. st. (first row k.) until work measures same as back, less 2 rows, to armhole shaping.

Pocket Opening
Next row: k.19(23:28:30:33), sl. next 24 sts. onto st. holder and k. across 24 sts. from pocket lining, k. to end.
P.1 row.

Shape Armhole
Cast off 5 sts. at beg. of next row.
P.1 row.
Dec. 1 st. at armhole edge on next 5 rows, then on every foll. alt. row 4(5:5:6:6) times. [42(45:49:52:54) sts.]
Cont. straight until armhole measures 12(13:13:14:15) cm. (4¾(5:5:5½:5¾) in.), ending with a k. row.

Shape Neck
Cast off 23(24:26:27:27) sts. at beg. of next row. [19(21:23:25:27) sts.]
Cont. straight until armhole measures same as back, ending with a p. row.

Shape Shoulder
Cast off 5(5:5:6:6) sts. at beg. of next and foll. 2 alt. rows.

Work 1 row.
Cast off rem. 4(6:8:7:9) sts.

CARDIGAN RIGHT FRONT

Work as for left front, reversing shapings and omitting pocket.

CARDIGAN SLEEVES

Cast on 70(74:78:82:86) sts. with 2¾mm. needles.
Work 20 rows in st. st.
Change to 3¼mm. needles.
Cont. in st. st. for 24 rows, ending with a p. row.
To reverse work:
Next row: p.
Beg. with a k. row, work 10 rows.
Inc. 1 st. at each end of next and every foll. 12th row 12 times in all. [94(98:102: 106:110) sts.]
Cont. straight until sleeve measures 44 cm. (17¼ in.) from reverse row.

Shape Top
Cast off 5 sts. at beg. of next 2 rows.
Dec. 1 st. at each end of next 7 rows, then every foll. alt. row until 46(50:54:56:60) sts. rem.
Dec. 1 st. at each end of next 10(12:14: 14:16) rows.
Cast off rem. 26(26:26:28:28) sts.

CARDIGAN POCKET TOP

With 2¾mm. needles and right side of work facing, k. across 24 sts. of pocket.
Work 18 rows in st. st.
Cast off.

CARDIGAN FRONT BANDS

Cast on 16 sts. with 2¾mm. needles.
Work in st. st. until band is long enough to fit up front to neck shaping, stretched slightly.

Mitre Corner
Dec. 1 st. at each end of next 7 rows. [2 sts.]
K.2 tog., fasten off.
Work another band to match.

CARDIGAN BACK & SIDE NECK BANDS

Sew up shoulder seams.
With 2¾mm. needles and right side facing, pick up 23 sts. along straight side edge of front neck to top shoulder, 56(58:60:62:64) sts. from spare needle at back, and 23 sts. down front neck. [102(104:106:108:110) sts.]
Now work in st. st., p. first row.
Dec. 1 st. at each end of next 8 rows.
Work 1 row.
Now inc. 1 st. at each end of next 8 rows.
Cast off.

CARDIGAN FRONT NECK BANDS

With 2¾mm. needles and right side of work facing, pick up 23(24:26:27:27) sts. from front neck of left front.
Now work in st. st., p. first row.
Dec. 1 st. at inner edge and inc. 1 st. at neck edge on next 8 rows.
Work 1 row.
Dec. 1 st. at neck edge and inc. 1 st. at inner edge on next 8 rows.
Cast off.
Work other side to match.

CARDIGAN MAKING UP

Press lightly on wrong side avoiding rib.
Set in sleeves.
Sew up side and sleeve seams to beg. of cuff, reverse work and complete seam.
Sew back, side and front bands in position.
Sew up all mitred corners.
Turn bands to inside and sew to seams.
Sew pocket lining in place.
Turn pocket top in half onto inside and sew in place, then sew edges of top in position.
Press seams.
Turn cuff to outside and press lightly in place.

SWEATER BACK

Cast on 120(126:134:140:148) sts. with 2¾mm. needles.
Work 24 rows in k.2, p.2 rib.
Change to 3¼mm. needles.
Cont. in st. st. (first row k.) until work measures 42(41:41:40:40) cm. (16½(16:16: 15¾:15¾) in.), ending with a p. row.

Shape Armholes
Cast off 5 sts. at beg. of next 2 rows.
Dec. 1 st. at each end of next 5 rows, then on every foll. alt. row 3(3:4:4:5) times. [94(100:106:112:118) sts.] *.
Cont. straight until armholes measure 18(19:19:20:20) cm. (7(7½:7½:7¾:7¾) in.), ending with a p. row.

Shape Shoulders
Cast off 5(5:5:6:6) sts. at beg. of next 6 rows and 4(6:8:7:9) sts. at beg. of next 2 rows. [56(58:60:62:64) sts.]
Change to 2¾mm. needles and work 18 rows in st. st.
Cast off.

SWEATER FRONT

Work as for back to *.
Cont. straight until armholes measure 11(12:12:13:13) cm. (4¼(4¾:4¾:5:5) in.), ending with a p. row.

Divide for Neck
1st row: k.19(21:23:25:27) sts., turn, leave rem. sts. on a spare needle.
Cont. on these 19(21:23:25:27) sts. until armhole measures same as back, ending with a p. row.

Shape Shoulder
Cast off 5(5:5:6:6) sts. at beg. of next and foll. 2 alt. rows.
Work 1 row.
Cast off rem. 4(6:8:7:9) sts.
Sl. centre 56(58:60:62:64) sts. onto a spare needle.
Rejoin yarn to rem. sts. and work to match first side, reversing shapings.

SWEATER SLEEVES

Cast on 60(62:64:66:68) sts. with 2¾mm. needles.
Work 24 rows in k.2, p.2 rib.

Change to 3¼mm. needles.
Cont. in st. st. (first row k.), work 6 rows.
Inc. 1 st. at each end of next and every foll. 8th(7th:7th:6th:6th) row, 16(17:18: 19:20) times in all. [92(96:100:104:108) sts.]
Cont. straight until sleeve measures 44 cm. (17¼ in.)

Shape Top
Cast off 5 sts. at beg. of next 2 rows.
Dec. 1 st. at each end of next 7 rows, then every foll. alt. row 12(12:12:13:13) times.
Dec. 1 st. at each end of next 8(10:12: 12:14) rows.
Cast off rem. 28(28:28:30:30) sts.

SWEATER SIDE NECKBAND

With 2¾mm. needles and right side of work facing, pick up 23 sts. along straight edge of right front to top of shoulder.
Cont. in st. st., p.1 row.
Dec. 1 st. at front neck edge on next 8 rows.
Work 1 row.
Now inc. 1 st. at same edge on next 8 rows.
Cast off.
Work other side to match.

SWEATER FRONT NECKBAND

With 2¾mm. needles and right side of work facing, k.56(58:60:62:64) sts. from spare needle.
P. 1 row.
Dec. 1 st. at each end of next 8 rows.
Work 1 row.
Inc. 1 st. at each end of next 8 rows.
Cast off.

SWEATER MAKING UP

Press lightly on wrong side avoiding rib.
Sew up shoulder and neckband seams.
Set in sleeves.
Sew up side and shoulder seams.
Sew up mitred corners on front, turn neckband in half onto inside and sew to seams.
Press seams.